AIR UNIVERSITY

AIR FORCE RESEARCH INSTITUTE

The Rise of Air Mobility and Its Generals

Laura L. Lenderman
Lieutenant Colonel, USAF

Drew Paper No. 1

Air University Press
Maxwell Air Force Base, Alabama 36112-5962

March 2008

Muir S. Fairchild Research Information Center Cataloging Data

Lenderman, Laura L.
    The rise of air mobility and its generals / Laura L. Lenderman.
      p. ; cm. – (Drew paper, 1941-3785 ; no. 1)
    Includes bibliographical references.
    ISBN 978-1-58566-175-6
      1. United States. Air Mobility Command—History. 2. United States. Air Force—General staff officers. 3. Airborne operations (Military science)—History. 4. Generals—United States—History. I. Title. II. Series.

    358.44/0973—dc22

First Printing March 2008
Second Printing April 2011

Disclaimer

Opinions, conclusions, and recommendations expressed or implied within are solely those of the author and do not necessarily represent the views of Air University, the United States Air Force, the Department of Defense, or any other US government agency. Cleared for public release: distribution unlimited.

This Drew Paper and others in the series are available electronically at the Air University Research Web site http://research.maxwell.af.mil and the AU Press Web site http://aupress.maxwell.af.mil.

The Drew Papers

The Drew Papers are occasional publications sponsored by the Air Force Research Institute (AFRI), Maxwell AFB, Alabama. This paper is the first in a new series AFRI is launching to commemorate the distinguished career of Col Dennis "Denny" Drew, USAF, retired. In 30 years at Air University, Colonel Drew served on the Air Command and Staff College faculty, directed the Airpower Research Institute, and served as dean, associate dean, and professor of military strategy at the School of Advanced Air and Space Studies, Maxwell AFB. Colonel Drew is one of the Air Force's most extensively published authors and an international speaker in high demand. He has lectured to over 100,000 students at Air University as well as to foreign military audiences. In 1985 he received the Muir S. Fairchild Award for outstanding contributions to Air University. In 2003 Queen Beatrix of the Netherlands made him a Knight in the Order of Orange-Nassau for his contributions to education in the Royal Netherlands Air Force.

The Drew Papers are dedicated to promoting the understanding of air and space power theory and application. These studies are published by the Air University Press and broadly distributed throughout the US Air Force, the Department of Defense, and other governmental organizations, as well as to leading scholars, selected institutions of higher learning, public-policy institutes, and the media.

All military members and civilian employees assigned to Air University are invited to contribute unclassified manuscripts that deal with air and/or space power history, theory, doctrine, or strategy, or with joint or combined service matters bearing on the application of air and/or space power.

Authors should submit three copies of a double-spaced, typed manuscript and an electronic version of the manuscript on removable media along with a brief (200-word maximum) abstract. The electronic file should be compatible with Microsoft Windows and Microsoft Word—Air University Press uses Word as its standard word-processing program.

Please send inquiries or comments to
Director
Air Force Research Institute
155 N. Twining St.
Maxwell AFB, AL 36112-6026
Tel: (334) 953-9587
DSN 493-9587
Fax: (334) 953-6739
DSN 493-6739
E-mail: research.support@maxwell.af.mil

Contents

Chapter		Page
	DISCLAIMER	ii
	FOREWORD	vii
	ABOUT THE AUTHOR	ix
	ACKNOWLEDGMENTS	xi
	INTRODUCTION	xiii
1	MAHAN AND THE PURPOSE OF AIRPOWER	1
	Notes	6
2	THE RISE OF MOBILITY OPERATIONS	9
	Notes	23
3	THE RISE OF MOBILITY GENERALS	27
	Notes	54
4	THE FUTURE OF MOBILITY GENERALS	61
	Notes	72
5	CONCLUSIONS	75
	Notes	77
	BIBLIOGRAPHY	79

Foreword

In the early years of the Cold War, the United States relied on strategic nuclear attack as the primary means of deterring the Soviet Union. The focus on manned bombers and atomic weapons led to the rise of Strategic Air Command and its leaders, the bomber generals, within the Air Force. The power and influence of the bomber generals peaked in the early 1960s. In the following two decades, Tactical Air Command and the power of fighter generals rose within the Air Force. Mike Worden described this transformation of leadership in his insightful book *Rise of the Fighter Generals: The Problem of Air Force Leadership, 1945–1982.* Worden argued that fighter pilots rose to preeminence over bomber pilots because the bomber generals failed to adjust to changing realities related to America's failure in Vietnam and a growing conventional Soviet threat. The transition was complete by 1982, when a fighter pilot, Gen Charles A. Gabriel, became Air Force chief of staff. Today, 25 years after first assuming top command, fighter pilots continue to lead the Air Force.

During the rise of the fighter generals, mobility operations played a significant yet secondary role in airpower strategy. Since the end of the Cold War, however, airlift, air-refueling, and aeromedical-evacuation missions flown in support of combat and humanitarian operations have become an indispensable and direct aspect of US grand strategy. Mobility missions now comprise the majority of sorties controlled by the combined air operations center at Al Udeid Air Base in Qatar. In fact, mobility missions flown in support of Operations Iraqi Freedom and Enduring Freedom outnumber fighter and bomber sorties two to one.

Mobility forces dominate air operations in the post–Cold War era, at least statistically. Colonel Lenderman examines this trend and finds that as the United States moved from a strategy of containment toward engagement throughout the world, a corresponding shift occurred—away from contingencies demanding heavy concentrations of fighter and bomber planes and toward myriad, complex operations demanding mobility aircraft. She also shows that as the number and importance of mobility-centric operations increased, the number of generals

FOREWORD

with mobility expertise also increased, especially at the most senior levels of the Air Force. The change in the composition of senior Air Force leaders is significant because it indicates that the Air Force is adapting to alterations in the geopolitical environment. It is important that we recognize and examine this change not only because it occurs infrequently within large bureaucratic organizations but also because it may signal a significant shift in the future direction of the Air Force.

Colonel Lenderman explores the increase in the number and influence of mobility generals in the late twentieth century and looks toward the future, presenting possible reasons why these generals will continue to rise or why their opportunities may be limited. She concludes by discussing the significance of this study as it pertains to the Air Force's development and the nation's security.

Originally submitted as a thesis for Air University's School of Advanced Air and Space Studies (SAASS), *The Rise of Air Mobility and Its Generals* won the 2007 Airlift Tanker Association Global Reach Award as the best SAASS thesis on air mobility.

DANIEL R. MORTENSEN
Chief of Research
Airpower Research Institute

About the Author

Lt Col Laura L. Lenderman wrote this paper as a student assigned to the School of Advanced Air and Space Studies (SAASS), Maxwell AFB, Alabama. Colonel Lenderman attended Duke University on a four-year ROTC scholarship and graduated with an electrical-engineering degree in 1993. After graduating from Duke, she attended undergraduate pilot training at Columbus AFB, Mississippi. Upon graduation, she received her assignment to the KC-135 Stratotanker, Grand Forks AFB, North Dakota. While stationed there, Colonel Lenderman was selected to attend the Air Force Intern Program at the Pentagon, Washington, DC. During her tour at the Pentagon, she earned her master's degree in organizational management from George Washington University. After graduating from the Intern Program, she returned to flying tankers at Fairchild AFB, Washington. While stationed at Fairchild, she was selected to perform duties as a presidential advance agent for *Air Force One* and the 89th Presidential Airlift Group.

Following the terrorist attacks of 11 September 2001, Colonel Lenderman deployed to the Middle East in support of Operation Enduring Freedom. Shortly after her return, she again deployed to support Operation Iraqi Freedom, where she served as assistant director of operations for the largest air-refueling operation in the area of responsibility, comprised of 30 aircraft and 193 personnel from six bases. Following the war, she moved to Altus AFB, Oklahoma, where she was assigned to the 54th Air Refueling Squadron. As an assistant director of operations in the Air Force's KC-135 Formal Training Unit, she supervised the flying activities of 70 instructors and managed the annual training of 600 aircrew members. Following her assignment at Altus, she attended Air Command and Staff College at Maxwell AFB, Alabama, where she was a distinguished graduate and winner of the Commandant's Leadership Award. Following the completion of her studies at SAASS, Colonel Lenderman assumed command of the 15th Air Mobility Operations Squadron at Travis AFB, California.

Acknowledgments

This year has been one of the most challenging and rewarding of my Air Force career. First, I thank my School of Advanced Air and Space Studies (SAASS) XVI classmates. I am honored to call them brothers and friends.

I am also thankful for the faculty and staff, whose professionalism and dedication to the SAASS mission are unsurpassed. My thesis adviser Dr. Thomas Hughes and reader Dr. Stephen Chiabotti deserve special recognition. Their intelligence and insight throughout the year were awe inspiring.

I am also deeply indebted to the numerous leaders and mentors who guided my development over the years. Col Tim Smith, Brig Gen Randal Fullhart, Brig Gen Scott Wuesthoff, and Col Tony Haney are responsible for providing me the guidance necessary to succeed in my career and life.

Most importantly, I would like to thank my family. I am especially grateful for the love and support of my husband, Maj Dave Lenderman, who fills my life with laughter. I also want to thank my mom, Marilou Cook, the best editor and friend—this thesis is as much hers as mine. Finally, I dedicate this paper to my dad, Col Gordon Cook—Vietnam veteran, air-mobility pilot, and the reason I am here today.

Introduction

Airpower includes a nation's ability to deliver cargo, people, and war-making potential through the air to a desired destination to accomplish a desired purpose.

—Gen Henry H. "Hap" Arnold

In the early years of the Cold War, the United States relied on strategic nuclear attack as the primary means of deterring the Soviet Union. The focus on manned bombers and atomic weapons led to the rise of Strategic Air Command (SAC) and its leaders, the bomber generals, within the Air Force. The power and influence of these generals peaked in the early 1960s. In the following two decades, Tactical Air Command (TAC) and the power of fighter generals rose within the Air Force. Mike Worden described this transformation of leadership in his insightful book *Rise of the Fighter Generals: The Problem of Air Force Leadership, 1945–1982.* Worden argued that fighter pilots rose to preeminence over bomber pilots because the bomber generals failed to adjust to changing realities related to America's failure in Vietnam and a growing conventional Soviet threat.[1] The transition was complete by 1982, when a fighter pilot, Gen Charles A. Gabriel, became Air Force chief of staff. Today, more than 25 years after first assuming top command, fighter pilots continue to lead the Air Force.

During the rise of the fighter generals, mobility operations played a significant yet secondary role in airpower strategy. Since the end of the Cold War, however, airlift, air-refueling, and aeromedical-evacuation missions flown in support of combat and humanitarian operations have become an indispensable and direct aspect of US grand strategy. Mobility missions now comprise the majority of sorties controlled by the combined air operations center at Al Udeid Air Base (AB) in Qatar.[2] In fact mobility missions flown in support of Operations Iraqi Freedom and Enduring Freedom outnumber fighter and bomber sorties two to one.[3] "Never before in the history of warfare have so many air missions during wartime been air mobility over such an extended period."[4] Besides supporting operations in the Middle East, mobility aircraft fly the preponderance of missions in two other major Air Force commands overseas. Mobility aircraft fly 90–95 percent of United States Air Forces in Europe (USAFE) and 90 percent of Pacific Air Forces (PACAF) missions.[5] The recent increase in mobility operations is part of a longer-term trend.[6] Thomas Barnett described the "trend towards mobility centric warfighting" in his book *The Pentagon's New Roadmap: War and Peace in the Twenty-first Century*.[7] According to Barnett, "from 1990–2003, 80% of the 143 contingencies the U.S. military executed were mobility centric."[8]

These figures indicate that mobility forces dominate air operations in the post–Cold War era, at least statistically. This paper examines this trend and finds that as the United States moved from a strategy of containment toward engagement throughout the world, there was a corresponding shift away from contingencies demanding heavy concentrations of fighter and bomber planes and toward myriad, complex operations demanding mobility aircraft. The paper also shows that as the number and importance of mobility-centric operations increased, the number of generals with mobility expertise also increased, especially at the most senior levels of the Air Force. For example, in 1997 one out of 11 four-star generals (9 percent) and three out of 36 three-star generals (8 percent) had a mobility background.[9] By 2007 two out of 12 four-star generals (16 percent) and 10 out of 40 three star-generals (25 percent) had mobility experience.[10] The change in the composition of senior Air Force leaders does not mean that the fighter and bomber communities are "out of business."[11] This could not be further from the truth. The world is a dangerous place, and kinetic airpower remains a critical aspect of national security strategy. Rather, the rise of mobility generals in the post–Cold War era indicates that the Air Force is changing "its internal organization to match a changing external environment," which benefits the Air Force and the nation writ large.[12] This change is important to recognize and examine not only because it occurs infrequently within large, bureaucratic organizations but also because it may signal a significant shift in the future direction of the Air Force. If this proves to be true, the rise of mobility generals will have an impact on the Air Force's future vision, doctrine, budget priorities, and acquisition programs.[13]

Chapter 1 of this paper explores the increase in the number and influence of mobility generals in the late twentieth century by presenting a theoretical foundation for their rise, based on Alfred Thayer Mahan's concept of sea power. Chapter 2 examines geopolitical changes in the post–Cold War era, which led to an increase in mobility operations. Chapter 3 reviews the unique mission expertise and worldview that air-mobility experts provide the nation. It also discusses organizational and cultural changes as well as Air Mobility Command's (AMC) leadership-development program, which prepares mobility leaders to assume increased responsibility. Chapter 4 looks toward the future, presenting possible reasons why mobility generals will continue to rise in prominence or why their opportunities may be limited. Chapter 5 concludes by discussing the study's significance as it pertains to the Air Force's development and the nation's security.

Notes

(All notes appear in shortened form. For full details, see the appropriate entry in the bibliography.)

1. Worden, "Changing of the Guard."
2. Bossert, "Global War on Terror (GWoT)," 18.
3. Shriver to the author, e-mail. The average daily sortie count from January 2003 to April 2006 was 220 sorties per day; 150 of the sorties each day were mobility sorties.
4. Bossert, "Global War on Terror (GWoT)," 18.
5. Ibid.
6. Ibid.
7. Quoted in ibid.
8. Quoted in ibid.
9. Smith, *USAF Culture and Cohesion*, 15.
10. United States Air Force Biographies Web site.
11. Bossert, "Global War on Terror (GWoT)," 18.
12. Danskine, "Fall of the Fighter Generals," 2.
13. Ibid.

Chapter 1

Mahan and the Purpose of Airpower

Logistics . . . as vital to military success as daily food is to daily work.

—Capt A. T. Mahan, *Armaments and Arbitration*, 1912

Navy captain Alfred Thayer Mahan's late-nineteenth-century theory of sea power resonated with many military and political leaders. In his most influential work, *The Influence of Sea Power upon History, 1660–1783*, Mahan posited a direct relationship between a nation's great-power status and its ability to achieve command of the sea. He advocated that great nations achieve command of the sea for a specific purpose—as a means to an end. That end was increased commercial trade to buttress the national interest.[1] For Mahan the sea was a great commons, and those nations that controlled the world's waterways would dominate the globe. Although several of his propositions are outdated or sometimes misinterpreted, Mahan still has much to offer twenty-first-century military strategists. This chapter discusses some of his most important ideas and describes how they offer insight into command of the air and the purpose of American airpower in the post–Cold War era.

Mahan wrote his treatise during a period of great change in the nation's history. In 1890 the United States' frontier officially closed, pushing further national expansion overseas.[2] Mahan's exhortations for naval growth captured the spirit of expansion and the imagination of leaders such as Theodore Roosevelt and others who wanted the United States to take its "rightful place in the assemblage of world powers."[3] By this time, too, America had mostly recovered from its great Civil War and was embracing the industrial revolution, which touched almost every aspect of American society, including the US Navy. Vast maritime technological changes occurred during this time, propelling the Navy from sailing vessels and wooden hulls to steam power and metal ships.[4] Although Mahan recognized the significance of these changes, he mostly employed naval history to flesh out a naval strategy for the nation. "Naval strategy has for its end," he wrote, "to found, support, and increase, as well in peace as in war, the sea power of a country."[5] Throughout his writing, he strove to explain the strategic purpose of building and maintaining a strong Navy, which he recognized would be a critical enabler for the extension of US influence beyond its borders. He believed that the very principles governing command of the sea and the purpose of the Navy were unaffected by technological change because, despite advances in ship technology, the "behavior of people" rarely changed throughout history.[6] "Finally," Mahan wrote, "it must be remembered that, among all changes, the nature of man remains much the same; the personal equation, though uncertain in quantity and quality in the particular instance, is sure always to be found."[7] Divorced from technological change and focused on strategy rather than tactics, Mahan's theories have withstood the test of time and are readily adaptable to the ideas governing the application of military force through other media, including the air.

One of Mahan's most enduring propositions was his notion that the sea is a great commons. Describing the sea from a political and social point of view, Mahan depicted it as "a great highway" and a "wide common, over which men may pass in all directions, but on which some well-worn paths show that controlling reasons have led them to choose certain lines of travel rather than others."[8] He realized that throughout most of history, the sea had presented itself, to those willing to use it, as the most efficient line of communications. Although his analysis relied on specialized geographic and technological circumstances, from the perspective of geopolitics, he was essentially correct. To become a great nation, the United States needed to be able to *use* the sea commons, and to use the sea, the nation needed to obtain and maintain command of the sea. This was the best way, Mahan argued, for the nation to protect the trade routes, which constituted the primary means of acquiring raw materials and access to markets abroad.[9] Without access to seaports and the commercial and military use of the sea lines of communications, the nation would not be able to grow and achieve its great-power status.[10]

Mahan believed that the Navy's primary purpose was to enable the nation to effectively use the sea to increase its trading and economic power. For him, the Navy's method would always be martial, but its intention was thoroughly broader. In other words, achieving command of the sea was "essentially a battle for communications, to secure them for oneself and deny them to the enemy."[11] This idea is lost on many readers of Mahan, who focus on how he advocated that the United States should "gain command of the sea through a great naval battle between capital ships."[12] But focusing on Mahan's insistence on decisive battle obscures his basic purpose. He probably stressed the great battle for specific reasons because the "concept of sea power was a subtle one, and like all subtle concepts, it had to be simplified in order to get it across to a wider audience."[13] As a result, the great military essayist Sir Michael Howard believed that the "concept of sea power became simplified into that of exercising *command* of the sea" (emphasis in original).[14] In the end, this tended to distort Mahan's true focus: "Command of the sea became regarded as an end in itself rather than a means for securing other ends—the purpose of the war."[15]

A thorough reading and understanding of Mahan reveals a comprehensive concept of sea power. Rather than focus on sea power solely in terms of the "naval might of a nation measured in terms of number, size, and weight of ships of the line, Mahan viewed sea power in the broad sense."[16] He recognized that sea power included "all that tends to make a people great upon the sea or by the sea."[17] Thus, a nation's sea power included all of its maritime resources, naval strength being just one of them. In addition to naval superiority, sea power included "that combination of maritime commerce, overseas possessions, and privileged access to foreign markets that produces national 'wealth and greatness.'"[18]

In describing the military and economic purpose of sea power, Mahan also highlighted the importance of wartime logistics, which he referred to as communications. He broadly defined communications as "lines of movement by which a military body . . . is kept in living connection with the national power" and also as "those necessaries, supplies of which the ships cannot carry in their own hull beyond a limited amount."[19] Throughout his writings, he stressed that successful maritime strategy and ultimately a nation's great-power status depended on the Navy's ability to protect the sea lines of communications and ensure the safe movement of supplies, men, and equipment over the seas.

Mahan's broad concept of sea power reverberates through Billy Mitchell's theory of airpower, which he outlined in his book *Winged Defense: The Development and Possibilities of Modern Air Power—Economic and Military* (1925). Writing 35 years after the publication of Mahan's greatest work, Mitchell foresaw the United States changing from a maritime to an airpower nation. He purported that the nation (and the world) was standing "on the threshold of the 'aeronautical era.'"[20] Although his immediate purpose in describing this new era was to advocate an independent Air Force by using, consciously or not, many of Mahan's basic concepts of sea power and applying them to the air, Mitchell presented a compelling, long-range vision of the future purpose of airpower.

Just as Mahan described the need for the United States to become a maritime nation in order to achieve great-nation status, so did Mitchell describe how the future of the United States was "indissolubly bound up in the development of air power."[21] Like Mahan, he acknowledged the importance of gaining command of the medium. Instead of a decisive battle at sea, however, Airmen would conduct great "air battles" in their pursuit of air supremacy.[22] Mitchell argued that the purpose of airpower was not solely the destruction of enemy air forces and the projection of military power. Rather, it was an instrument of national policy, just as the Navy was for Mahan. Although air battles were important, Mitchell recognized that they were a means to an end, which, for him, was the unfettered use of the air in order to achieve national interests. Mitchell explained that airpower served a higher purpose and that his goal was to show how best to use the air for the object of war.[23] His definition of airpower captured the strategic importance of this view: the "ability to do something in the air. It consists of transporting all sorts of things by aircraft from one place to another, and as air covers the whole world there is no place that is immune from influence by aircraft."[24] Like readers of Mahan, many devotees of Mitchell allowed the means championed to obscure the ends about which he wrote. Mitchell certainly wanted capable fleets of fighters and bomber planes. He surely believed that the nation must develop great competence in air battle. He believed to his dying breath in an independent air arm. But none of this was the essential purpose of his effort.

Like Mahan, who described the relationship between the military and commercial aspects of sea power, Mitchell noted a similar relationship regarding airpower. He described air as a "common medium all over the world" and purported that development of a robust commercial aviation industry and transportation system was a critical element of airpower.[25] "No matter how great a producer or manufacturer a nation may be, if it has no means of transportation it cannot distribute its goods or gain the benefits which come from other nations."[26] He determined that "the substantial and continual development of air power should be based on sound commercial aviation."[27]

Mitchell was writing well ahead of his time in the 1920s. Over the next 70 years, commercial and military airpower came of age, and the United States eventually fulfilled Mitchell's vision. By the 1990s, most commercial travel was by air.[28] In addition, "more and more goods are shipped by air," most "communications are routed through satellites, and the largest segment of US exports comes from the aerospace industry."[29] Likewise, military airpower has become the cornerstone of national defense. "Land and naval forces cannot operate effectively in the absence of air superiority by friendly forces. With control of the skies, airmen can deliver devastating blows to enemy land and naval forces orchestrated in joint campaigns."[30] The growth and pervasiveness of airpower reveals that "first and foremost . . . the United States is an aerospace nation."[31]

For most of the twentieth century, decisive air battles overshadowed the ultimate purpose of airpower. In the pursuit of air dominance in the twenty-first century, it behooves air strategists to recall the teachings of Mitchell and his purpose. Just as in his day, gaining control of the air is not the ultimate goal; it is how the nation uses control of the air. Now is the time to utilize control of the airways effectively. The nation is once again standing at the precipice of great change. The end of the Cold War and the onset of the global war on terror (GWOT) may well be as monumental a shift as the closing of the frontier a century ago. Air dominance is the means to specific ends, one of which is the free and safe movement of supplies, troops, and equipment to achieve national interests. Today the air is the great commons, and the United States is an air and space nation. The country's civilian air assets, which include large passenger airlines and robust freight operations, sit at the center of this reality. In the United States Air Force, however, the mobility community is most poised to leverage this capability in communications underwritten by the combat air forces (CAF). When one considers the factor of time, the air now presents the most efficient line of communications. This, then, is the reason why the Air Force is nurturing and sustaining men and women with air-mobility competencies—and should continue to do so.

Notes

1. McDowell, "Mahan, Sea Power, and Air Power," 3.
2. Mets, "Fodder for Your Professional Reading," 68.
3. McDowell, "Mahan, Sea Power, and Air Power," 4.
4. Mets, "Fodder for Your Professional Reading," 68.
5. Mahan, *Influence of Sea Power upon History*, 89.
6. Parrish, "Influence of Air Power upon Historians."
7. Quoted in ibid.
8. Mahan, *Influence of Sea Power upon History*, 25.
9. Ibid.
10. Ibid.
11. McDowell, "Mahan, Sea Power, and Air Power," 22.
12. Mets, "Fodder for Your Professional Reading," 68.
13. Howard, "Concept of Air Power," 6.
14. Ibid.
15. Ibid., 7.
16. McDowell, "Mahan, Sea Power, and Air Power," 9.
17. Mahan, *Influence of Sea Power upon History*, 1.
18. Crowl, "Alfred Thayer Mahan," 451.
19. Quoted in ibid., 460.
20. Mitchell, *Winged Defense*, 1.
21. Ibid., ix.
22. Ibid., 9.
23. Howard, "Concept of Air Power," 8.
24. Mitchell, *Winged Defense*, xii.
25. Ibid., 78.
26. Ibid., 77.
27. Ibid., 96.
28. Fogleman, "Aerospace Nation." Civilian airline travel in the United States has increased dramatically, especially in the post–Cold War era. Annual passenger travel by means of domestic airlines increased fourfold between 1964 and 1993. Federal Aviation Administration, "Aviation System Capacity Annual Report," 4. By 2005 "739 million people flew U.S. commercial carriers,

compared to 580 million in 1995, and 382 million in 1985. The FAA [Federal Aviation Administration] expects this figure to reach 1 billion people by 2015." Federal Aviation Administration Air Traffic Organization, "Moving America Safely," 10.

29. Fogleman, "Aerospace Nation." Besides increased passenger air travel, the commercial airfreight industry has grown dramatically over the years. In 1970 US commercial air carriers totaled 4.6 million revenue-ton-miles compared to 32.8 million revenue-ton-miles in 2003. "Air Cargo Statistics."

30. Drew, "We Are an Aerospace Nation," 34.

31. Ibid.

Chapter 2

The Rise of Mobility Operations

Without air mobility, we would have the best continental defense in the world. Air mobility allows us to move beyond our borders and conduct US national security policy anywhere in the world.

—Lt Gen John Sams
Commander, Fifteenth Air Force

When the United States emerged as a global power as well as an air and space nation in the second half of the twentieth century, national leaders recognized the importance of projecting military power rapidly anywhere in the world. As early as World War II, airlift and, later, air-refueling capabilities were critical to American power projection throughout a broad spectrum of operations, from humanitarian assistance to armed conflict.[1] Air-mobility capabilities became especially relevant as the British and French empires declined between 1945 and 1965, and the United States stepped in to fill the void and contain communism in many places around the world.[2] The demand to deploy rapidly and sustain forces increased dramatically in the post–Cold War era. For example, the Air Force took part in 60 deployments in 1990 and by 1997 had tallied over 600 deployments across the full spectrum of operations.[3] This trend intensified after the terror attacks of 11 September 2001 (9/11). In today's complex, uncertain world, air mobility is "the 'linchpin' of American national security" and national security policy.[4] This chapter explores this proposition by providing historical context and describing several air-mobility operations from 1942 to 1991. It then examines geopolitical changes in the post–Cold War era and analyzes how those changes and the attacks of 9/11 altered the international security environment. In the process, this chapter reveals that revolutionary changes in the global security environment over the last 15 years have placed an ever-greater premium on air-mobility forces and capabilities.

Air-Mobility Operations from World War II to the End of the Cold War

We have learned and must never forget that from now on air transport is an essential element of airpower, in fact of all national power.

—Gen Henry H. "Hap" Arnold, 1945

Although military-transport forces grew steadily throughout the 1920s and 1930s, air mobility rapidly came of age during World War II. Most notably, airlift operations flown from Burma and India over the Himalayan Mountains into China in 1942–45 provided a lifeline to American and Chinese forces that was critical to the Allied strategy of keeping China in the war.[5] The airlift missions flown over "the Hump" were important because the Allies planned to use China as a future staging base for an invasion of Japan and also needed "to keep Japanese forces (over 1.2 million men) tied up in China to reduce their strength in other South Pacific areas."[6] This ambitious operation, which comprised 167,285 missions and delivered 740,000 tons of supplies, began "a new era of air power" and was a preview of the strategic impact that air mobility had during the Cold War.[7]

The Berlin blockade helped mark the beginning of the Cold War and set the stage for one of the most celebrated air-mobility operations. The Soviets began the blockade on 24 June 1948 by cutting off "all surface transportation between Berlin and the Western Occupation Zones of Germany."[8] At that time, Western leaders could afford neither a confrontation with the Soviets nor abandonment of the city. So they decided to resupply Berlin by air. During the Berlin airlift, air-mobility forces flew 276,926 sorties and delivered 2,323,067 tons of supplies to the city until the Soviets abandoned the blockade on 12 May 1949.[9] The C-47s and C-54s became symbols of hope and freedom for the people of Berlin. More broadly, the first battle of the Cold War ended without either side firing a shot and "led to the notion that sometimes the nonlethal forms of airpower could directly achieve national objectives."[10]

Following the Berlin airlift, air mobility continued to play a critical role in achieving national security objectives, especially when the Cold War turned hot during the Vietnam War. The battle of Khe Sanh offers an example of the profound impact of tactical-mobility forces on combat. During the battle in January 1968, 15,000 North Vietnamese troops surrounded three Marine battalions at a remote outpost near the demilitarized zone in South Vietnam.[11] During the four-month siege, American forces relied on C-130s and C-123s to reinforce and resupply the base. Both the location of the base in a valley and poor weather challenged the airlift crews.[12] The North Vietnamese controlled the high ground and "kept up a deadly crossfire that prevented the C-130s from landing at Khe Sanh and severely limited C-123 operations."[13] Meanwhile, the poor weather prevented strike aircraft from attacking the enemy surrounding Khe Sanh. Airlift crews overcame these challenges by using innovative tactical-arrival procedures and off-loading techniques to sustain the marines. By March the weather had improved enough to allow effective air strikes against the North Vietnamese positions. By the time the battle ended in April 1968, the enemy had destroyed three C-123s and damaged 18 C-130s and eight C-123s.[14] Nonetheless, the air bridge succeeded in sustaining the outpost throughout the siege. Altogether, mobility aircrews flew 1,128 missions and delivered 12,430 tons of materials to the beleaguered troops at Khe Sanh.[15]

Besides highlighting tactical airlift, the Vietnam War was also the proving ground for air refueling. Tankers were critical to the defeat of North Vietnam's spring offensive in 1972. In less than a week, air refuelers created an air bridge and moved an entire fighter wing of F-4s and F-105s from Holloman Air Force Base (AFB) in New Mexico to Takhli AB in Thailand.[16] The tankers enabled the "rapid reinforcement of the in-theater forces" and helped defeat the enemy's offensive operations.[17] Air refueling was also vital to the success of the B-52 operations over North Vietnam, especially in December 1972. After the North Vietnamese walked out of peace negotiations on 13 December, the United States launched Linebacker II and resumed bombing North Vietnam in order to force the enemy back to the peace table. The KC-135s were "essential to the success of the B-52 and fighter operations. Without the tankers, the 6,000-mile bomber mission from Guam would have been impossible."[18] Although South Vietnam eventually fell to the communists, airlift and air refueling proved an invaluable means of power projection throughout the conflict.

As the Vietnam War drew to a close, air-mobility operations helped shape the Yom Kippur War. Soon after the conflict among Israel, Egypt, and Syria began in 1973, Israeli forces started running out of tanks as well as ammunition and called on the United States for aid.[19] Pres. Richard Nixon ordered air-mobility forces to resupply Israel in an operation dubbed Nickel Grass.[20] In record time, C-5s and C-141s were in the air and en route to the Middle East. The airlift had significant military and political effects. It not only resupplied the Israelis with needed equipment and demonstrated the effectiveness of US strategic air assets but also had far-reaching impact in terms of US relations with Israel, the Soviet Union, Arab countries, and the North Atlantic Treaty Organization.[21] The operation also "supported the contention that airlift may be among the most flexible options available to the national command authorities . . . for the execution of national policy during peace or war."[22] By the end of the 30-day operation, air-mobility crews had flown 567 missions, delivered 22,318 tons of supplies, and helped save Israel from impending defeat.[23] "For generations to come," Israeli prime minister Golda Meir recalled of Nickel Grass, "all will be told of the miracle of the immense planes from the U.S. bringing in the material that meant life to our people."[24]

The Israeli airlift was but one example of air-mobility forces supporting national security policy during the last two decades of the Cold War. In the fall of 1983, the United States conducted Operation Urgent Fury in response to growing unrest in Grenada. National leaders called on Military Airlift Command (MAC) to evacuate Americans from the country as well as airdrop Army troops to secure the island. Five years later, mobility planes were also vital to the success of Operation Just Cause, which resulted in the successful capture of Panamanian dictator Manuel Noriega and restored democracy to the country. Throughout this operation, mobility forces "flew 775 missions to transport 39,994 passengers and 20,675 tons of cargo to and from Panama."[25]

These operations paled in comparison to the tremendous impact that air-mobility assets had during the crisis in the Gulf region in 1990 and 1991. Air-mobility forces were critical to the success of Operations Desert Shield and Desert Storm. Less than 24 hours after Iraq invaded Kuwait on 2 August 1990, a C-141 arrived in Saudi Arabia and began delivering troops and supplies to the region.[26] This flight marked the beginning of a five-month buildup of troops and war materials that culminated in mobility forces creating "a massive air bridge" and moving the equivalent of a small city to the desert.[27] The airlift moved "ten times the daily ton-miles of the 1948–1949 Berlin Airlift and four times that of the 1973 airlift to Israel."[28] According to Gen Hansford T. Johnson, commander of United States Transportation Command (USTRANSCOM) and MAC/Air Mobility Command (AMC), "We moved, in essence, a Midwestern town the size of Lafayette, Indiana, or Jefferson City, Missouri. In addition, we also moved the equivalent of all their cars, trucks, foodstuffs, stocks, household goods and water supply."[29]

Although intertheater airlift was critical to the success of the operation, tactical airlift also played a key role. The day after the air war began on 17 January 1991, C-130s secretly began moving an entire corps of 14,000 Army personnel across the desert in order to prepare for Gen Norman Schwarzkopf's "left hook," "an end-around maneuver designed to trap many Iraqi units and render them ineffective."[30] When the war ended and Saddam Hussein withdrew his forces from Kuwait, air-mobility assets began a six-month process of redeploying troops and supplies back to the United States. Throughout the crisis, air-mobility forces were vital to the success of the operation. Those forces not only enabled the rapid projection of US military power to the region but also sustained our personnel throughout the largest military operation since the Vietnam War.

The US Security Environment in the 1990s

In the emerging post–Cold War world, international relations promise to be more complicated, more volatile and less predictable. Indeed, of all the mistakes that could be made about the security challenges of a new era, the most dangerous would be to believe that suddenly the future can be predicted with certainty.

—Pres. George H. W. Bush, 1991

THE RISE OF MOBILITY OPERATIONS

> *We must be the world's premier deployer.*
> —Gen John Shalikashvili, 1997

The Gulf War was not the only US victory in the early 1990s. The liberation of Kuwait coincided with the collapse of the Soviet Union and the end of the Cold War. But while the United States basked in the glow of its victories in the Gulf and the Cold War, the rapid collapse of communism quickly ushered in an era of uncertainty. Although the end of the Cold War signaled the triumph of democracy, human rights, and free markets, America struggled throughout the 1990s to come to terms with its status as the world's lone superpower and the responsibility that came with the title.[31] The United States soon realized that the Soviet Union was not the originator of all of the world's problems.[32] While "communism left a bitter legacy in Eastern Europe, Russia, and Eurasia" and sometimes doomed old satellites to "interethnic tension, national rivalry, and despair," America also had to deal increasingly with "revolution, war, and famine" in noncommunist parts of the world as well as continue to contain Saddam's regime in Iraq.[33] As a result, American leaders struggled to chart a course and establish a role for their country in the world throughout the 1990s. In time, as the geopolitical environment changed, so did "the willingness of the United States to intervene in various crises around the world."[34] In particular, after the fall of the Soviet Union and free from possible communist reprisals, the United States became involved in more small-scale contingencies. As a result, US national security strategy called on air-mobility forces to support an increasing number of humanitarian and military operations around the world during the 1990s.

As the events in the Gulf unfolded and the Soviet Union imploded, Pres. George H. W. Bush focused on developing a new vision for American national policy. Unlike the situation during the previous four decades, when the United States focused on a single enemy, it no longer had to contend with a looming threat or guiding principle in the early post–Cold War security environment.[35] Bush acknowledged the lack of "an intellectual blueprint" to shape US policy in 1990 when he said, "There are no maps to lead us where we are going in this new world of our own making."[36] Although American leaders did not want to return to the brink of nuclear holocaust, the Cold War did provide focus for American policy as well as keep "the lid on other tensions which existed within and between states."[37] Bush hoped that his vision of a New World Order, which he outlined in a speech at the United Nations in October 1990, would fill the void and provide direction in the post–Cold War security environment.[38] Inspired by the cooperation among diverse nations leading up to the Gulf War, Bush envisioned "a new partnership of nations that transcends the cold war; a partnership based on consultation, cooperation and collective action . . . whose goals are to increase democracy, increase prosperity, increase the peace and reduce arms."[39] Additionally, Bush saw the United States taking the lead in the New World Order and recognized that instead of preparing to defeat a single enemy, the "US must prepare to meet regional threats 'in whatever corner of the globe they may occur.'"[40]

Bush further outlined his vision of the future in his *National Security Strategy (NSS)*, published shortly after the Gulf War. Importantly, he recognized that international relations would be "more complicated, more volatile and less predictable" in the post–Cold War world.[41] Likewise, in this new era, the United States planned to draw down its military forces by 25 percent and depend less on the forward basing of troops and more on establishing a forward presence wherever crisis or contingency required. This new posture relied on a robust air-mobility system to respond rapidly to developing crises.[42] "In this new era," the *NSS* proclaimed, "the ability to project our power will underpin our strategy more than ever. We must be able to deploy substantial forces and sustain them in parts of the world where prepositioning of equipment will not always be feasible, where adequate bases may not be available (at least before a crisis), and where there is a less developed industrial base and infrastructure to support our forces once they have arrived."[43]

Bush did not have much time to implement this vision because William J. Clinton defeated him in the presidential election of 1992. But Bush had been largely correct about new challenges around the world. In the early 1990s, the international community was dissolving into a state of chaos in some areas such as Yugoslavia and Somalia.[44] The violence in Central Europe and East Africa—and the lack of international consensus on the proper response to it—revealed that Bush's vision of a new era of peace and cooperation among nations could not "be extrapolated into a set of guiding principles for the post–Cold War period."[45] Compounding matters, the sources of conflict were increasingly complex, and wars seemed to occur more often "within rather than among nations."[46] These types of conflict made it difficult for US leaders to determine when and why America should intervene.

Soon after his election, President Clinton and his advisers assessed the security environment and determined that the threats to the United States would be even broader than Bush had anticipated.[47] Clinton's *NSS* of 1994 explained that "'not all security threats are military in nature' and that 'transnational phenomena such as terrorism, narcotics trafficking, environmental degradation, rapid population growth and refugee flows also have security implications.'"[48] In this new security environment, the Clinton administration developed a strategy of "engagement and enlargement," which recognized the importance of US leadership in the international community, especially in terms of promoting American economic prosperity.[49] The administration saw the end of the Cold War, according to Anthony Lake, Clinton's national security adviser, as an opportunity to "enlarge" the number of market democracies in the world.[50] According to the strategy, the United States "would strive to maintain a strong defense capability and promote cooperative security measures; work to open foreign markets; spur global economic growth; and promote democracy abroad."[51]

Changes in the international security environment described in Clinton's strategy of engagement and enlargement consequently drove changes in military strategy and force structure. In terms of the latter, the thawing of the Cold War resulted in a dramatic decrease in the number of military forces and overseas bases in the early 1990s. This, in turn, tended to accentuate the need for robust air-mobility forces to move combat troops to any number of hot spots throughout the world.[52]

The *National Military Strategy (NMS)* of 1995 reflected the military's growing focus on regional conflicts versus a global strategy of containment. According to the *NMS*, "Regional instabilities are, and will remain, a recurring challenge, from nations that implode into internal conflicts . . . to attacks against neighboring states. Many antagonisms that were buried by frozen relationships of the Cold War have now surfaced, adding to those that carried over from that era."[53] Security analysts Wyn Q. Bowen and David H. Dunn described two types of regional threats facing the United States in the post–Cold War era. The first type was a regional threat, such as Iraq, that directly threatened US vital interests.[54] The second type was a threat, such as Somalia, that stemmed "from religious, ethnic, nationalistic and other regional tensions which, although not directly threatening vital American interests, jeopardise what former Secretary of Defense Les Aspin called the 'American sense of decency.'"[55] The US military had to prepare for both types of regional threats, and this requirement demanded more flexibility and a broader array of capabilities compared to those needed during the Cold War.

Against this backdrop of changes to the security environment, military strategy, and force structure, fundamental organizational changes occurred within the Air Force in the 1990s. Air Force leaders recognized that changes in the security environment called for dramatic organizational changes within the service. Previously organized along strategic and tactical missions, this organizational structure no longer made sense as the Cold War thawed and as events in the Gulf War transpired.[56] In 1992 the Air Force reorganized SAC, TAC, and MAC into two major commands (MAJCOM): Air Combat Command (ACC) and AMC.[57] Henceforth, ACC owned the fighters and bombers, while AMC owned most of the airlift and tanker assets.[58] This constituted the most significant restructuring of the Air Force since the establishment of the service in 1947, and it enabled the Air Force to achieve more efficiently and effectively its vision of global reach/global power. In the new security environment that required the United States to respond rapidly to regional threats and humanitarian crises, mobility assets in AMC provided the global reach, while combat forces in ACC provided the global power.

As the 1990s unfolded, however, air mobility not only enabled airpower's reach but also, in many instances, represented the only source of American power in a number of humanitarian and peacekeeping operations. Throughout this period, na-

THE RISE OF MOBILITY OPERATIONS

tional leaders increasingly called on air-mobility personnel and assets to implement the strategy of engagement. The result was a staggering tempo of operations. "As the United States reduced its forward presence, but not its commitments in the post–Cold War setting, possessing the means to transport mobility forces rapidly assumed a larger importance."[59] Air-mobility forces were involved in a significant number of humanitarian operations such as the Somalia and Rwanda relief efforts, show-of-force missions like Uphold Democracy in Haiti, and combat operations in Bosnia, Kosovo, and the Middle East. In both temporal and spatial terms, these mobility operations differed from earlier ones by an order of magnitude. In 1997, for instance, AMC traveled to all but five of the world's countries, and three of those five did not have a runway.[60]

Mobility forces arrived shortly after disaster occurred and the world called for help. Even a cursory review reveals the increased reliance on and importance of air-mobility forces in the post–Cold War era. Their participation in small-scale contingencies, for instance, increased from 11 percent of AMC's operations in the 1980s to 32 percent in the 1990s.[61] In 1994 alone, AMC flew 850,000 passengers and carried 237,000 tons of cargo, making for monthly averages greater than those at the height of the Gulf War crisis just three years earlier.[62] Moreover, AMC participated in "167 humanitarian operations assisting 74 countries from 1990 to 1996, which comprised 12 percent of US military operations."[63] On top of all this, international peacekeeping missions had also increased since the end of the Cold War. For example, of the 46 United Nations peacekeeping operations between 1948 and 1999, 35 of them occurred after 1988.[64] Because countries now expect US involvement in these types of operations, the international community will continue to call on mobility forces for support whenever the need arises.[65]

The increase in operations in the late 1990s called for additional organizational changes in the Air Force. As a result, the service adopted an expeditionary air and space forces (EAF) concept that further emphasized the flexibility of air-mobility forces.[66] According to Gen Michael E. Ryan, Air Force chief of staff at the time, "The U.S. Air Force is no longer a Cold War garrison force focused on containment. The paradigm has shifted to a world that requires rapid and tailored engagement in many regions and many situations."[67] For the chief of staff and others, air mobility was critical to the ongoing success of the EAF and was "essential to seizing the initiative rapidly, containing conflict, and resolving the situation on terms favorable to the United States."[68] Importantly, the EAF concept acknowledged a new security environment that called for the capability to project military power rapidly, anywhere in the world. Whether engaged in humanitarian or combat operations, air mobility in the 1990s became a primary "means of demonstrating U.S. resolve" and was the key to the national security strategy of engagement in the early post–Cold War years.[69]

The US Security Environment after 9/11

Uncertainty is the defining characteristic of today's strategic environment. We can identify trends but cannot predict specific events with precision. . . . Our role in the world depends on effectively projecting and sustaining our forces in distant environments where adversaries may seek to deny us access.

—The National Defense Strategy of
the United States of America, 2005

Power is increasingly defined, not by mass or size, but by mobility and swiftness.

—Pres. George W. Bush

The pervasive uncertainty in the early post–Cold War international security environment was a prelude to the unpredictability of the post-9/11 geopolitical environment. The shocking terrorist attacks against the United States ushered in a new era of conflict. Rogue nations, terrorist groups, and America's longtime adversaries in the Middle East now became the focus of US foreign policy and defense strategy. Following the attacks, America engaged in combat on several fronts while also responding to calls for humanitarian relief around the world. After US forces achieved initial success in combat operations in Afghanistan, the nation's leaders struggled to chart a course for America and determine an appropriate long-term response in the new security environment. But whatever course US officials charted in the new era, the president and secretary of defense continued to call increasingly on air-mobility forces to implement American policy and achieve national goals around the world.

A year after the terrorist attacks on 9/11, President Bush published a new *NSS*. The attacks made combating terrorism a new focus for the United States. In particular, the new strategy emphasized the preemptive and preventive use of force as a means of protecting the United States from future attacks. The administration adopted the policy of preemption because it believed that the "continued spread of weapons of mass destruction (WMD) technology to states with a history of aggression creates an unacceptable level of risk" to the United States.[70] Therefore, the Bush administration declared that "'as a matter of common sense and self defense, America will act against [such] emerging threats before they are fully formed.'"[71] The new policy drew criticism from many analysts who believed that the United States would be more apt to use military force "'outside the bounds of international law and legitimacy'" in the future.[72] US policy came under further attack following the invasion of Iraq in 2003. Suspecting that Iraq maintained a well-developed WMD capability, the United States led a small coalition of nations and overthrew the Iraqi government. Following the invasion, however, inspectors found no WMDs, which fueled international criticism about the legitimacy of the invasion. Complicating matters, after major combat operations ended, Iraq quickly dissolved into a state of chaos and violence, which continues today.

The changes in the international security environment that drove the policy of preemption also fueled changes in military strategy in the post-9/11 era. The *NMS* published in 2004 focused on developing the military capabilities to fight the war on terror. Specifically, the strategy recognized that military forces must protect the homeland, prevent conflict and surprise attack, and ultimately prevail against a wider range of adversaries.[73] Beyond that, it placed a premium on the ability to project power rapidly around the world. In particular, the *NMS* called for strategic agility and for military forces to "retain the ability to contend with the principal characteristic of the security environment—uncertainty. Agility is the ability to rapidly deploy, employ, sustain, and redeploy capabilities in geographically separated and environmentally diverse regions."[74] Likewise, the *Quadrennial Defense Review Report* of 2006 emphasized the importance of speed and global mobility in the new security environment. According to the report, "Rapid global mobility is central to the effectiveness of the future force. The joint force will balance speed of deployment with desired warfighter effects to deliver the right capabilities at the right time and at the right place."[75]

The changes in the strategic environment and shifts in the national and military strategies had important implications for the employment of mobility forces in the post-9/11 era. Today, the president and secretary of defense continue to call increasingly on mobility forces to respond rapidly to developing crises in the uncertain strategic environment of the twenty-first century. Air mobility continues to be the backbone of "modern US expeditionary operations," and air-mobility assets are involved in all of the major operations in the GWOT as well as many humanitarian and peacekeeping operations around the world.[76] Immediately after the terrorist attacks, for instance, air-refueling planes began flying Operation Noble Eagle missions in support of homeland security. Elsewhere, tankers extensively supported operations in the Afghanistan theater of operations because combat aircraft had to fly hundreds of miles to and from their bases throughout Enduring Freedom. That operation also called for an extensive amount of airlift and saw the first "combat employment of the C-17 in an airland operation" to seize a forward operating base in southern Afghanistan.[77] Significantly, C-17s also executed humanitarian-relief operations during combat and air-dropped supplies to the Afghan people. The C-17s were the only means of delivering this relief because the Taliban had cut off ground routes for supplies. Consequently, air mobility achieved a "diplomatic, political, and military victory" during Enduring Freedom.[78] "For the first time in the history of war," Secretary of the Air Force James G. Roche said, "this country has fought in a land-locked area [Afghanistan] where every single thing going in and coming out has gone by air. Food, water, ammunition, troops were all transported by air, and that's really incredible."[79]

Air mobility continues to be equally impressive during ongoing operations in Iraq. As combat operations drew down in 2003–4, air-mobility operations increased. Not only does air mobility transport patients and the wounded from the theater but also it conducts most of the convoy operations for the Army.[80] Instead of transporting supplies and personnel by land, C-130s and C-17s fly most of the materials and people throughout the theater. Of approximately 200 sorties flown each day in Iraq, two-thirds of them are mobility sorties. The statistics quickly add up. By September 2006, after five years of combat and combat-support missions for the GWOT, AMC had flown more than "788,000 sorties, moved 6.44 million passengers, and delivered 3.9 billion pounds of fuel."[81] Additionally, in 2006, airlift operations in support of the wars in Afghanistan and Iraq surpassed the Berlin airlift and became the largest such operation in history.[82] President Bush's recent announcement to increase the number of troops in Iraq by 20,000 indicates that airlift operations and the movement of supplies in the theater will only increase in the future.

Besides combat operations in the Middle East, air-mobility platforms simultaneously supported peacetime humanitarian operations such as tsunami-relief missions in Indonesia in 2004, Hurricane Katrina support missions in 2005, and relief operations following a devastating earthquake in Pakistan in 2005. Today, it is unquestionably in America's interest to support these types of operations. In fact, "humanitarian responses are not only what *ought* to be done but also what *must* be done to minimize the risk to American soldiers and support the stable and upward development of the U.S. economy" (emphasis in original).[83]

This chapter examined several instances in which air mobility played a key role in implementing national policy. Air mobility served the nation well during the Cold War. Changes in the geopolitical environment, especially after 9/11, only increased demand on air-mobility forces and the capability they provide the nation and its allies. In fact, air-mobility forces are currently supporting "the longest sustained air mobility surge" in US history.[84] Today's world is complex and uncertain, and the US national security strategy depends now more than ever on the speed and flexibility of air-mobility forces to achieve political-military objectives. "The overarching strategy of our nation is forward defense," according to Gen Duane H. Cassidy, former MAC commander, "which implies you need transportation to get to the battle. If you're doing some retrenching and regressing from forward deployed forces, then you need transportation all the more. . . . You can build masses of F-15s, F-16s, and B-2s, but you're not going to take any land with them. You take territory with ground troops. Thus the key to our strategy must be transportation."[85] In the post–Cold War environment, therefore, rapid air mobility is truly the linchpin that enables policy makers to respond to crises developing around the world and across the full spectrum of operations—anytime, anywhere.

Notes

1. Smith, *Anything, Anywhere, Anytime*, iii.
2. Hutcheson, *Air Mobility*, 100.
3. Ibid., viii.
4. Ibid.
5. Ibid., 7–8.
6. Ibid., 7.
7. Ibid., 8.
8. Ibid., 12.
9. Ibid., 14.
10. Mets, "Between Two Worlds," 45.
11. Hutcheson, *Air Mobility*, 17.
12. Smith, *Anything, Anywhere, Anytime*, 134.
13. Ibid.
14. Ibid.
15. Hutcheson, *Air Mobility*, 18. The marines abandoned the base at Khe Sanh in July 1968 because they no longer needed a fixed operating base in that part of the country.
16. Ibid., 15.
17. Ibid.
18. Ibid., 17.
19. Ibid., 22.
20. See Krisinger, "Operation Nickel Grass."
21. Ibid., 18.
22. Ibid.
23. Hutcheson, *Air Mobility*, 23.
24. Quoted in ibid.
25. Smith, *Anything, Anywhere, Anytime*, 198.
26. Hutcheson, *Air Mobility*, 24.
27. Ibid., 25.
28. Ibid., 50.

29. Quoted in ibid., 25.
30. Ibid., 27.
31. Schulzinger, *U.S. Diplomacy since 1900*, 14.
32. Ibid., 13.
33. Ibid.
34. Hutcheson, *Air Mobility*, xiv.
35. Bowen and Dunn, *American Security Policy*, 8.
36. Quoted in ibid.
37. Ibid., 9.
38. Ibid., 10.
39. Quoted in ibid.
40. Ibid., 11.
41. *National Security Strategy of the United States*.
42. Hutcheson, *Air Mobility*, 38.
43. *National Security Strategy of the United States*.
44. Bowen and Dunn, *American Security Policy*, 12.
45. Ibid.
46. Lake, "From Containment to Enlargement."
47. Bowen and Dunn, *American Security Policy*, 24.
48. Quoted in ibid.
49. Ibid., 23.
50. Lake, "From Containment to Enlargement."
51. History, Air Mobility Command, vol. 1, 1 June 1992–31 December 1994, 312.
52. Aspin, *Report on the Bottom-Up Review*.
53. *National Military Strategy of the United States*, 1995.
54. Bowen and Dunn, *American Security Policy*, 38.
55. Ibid.
56. History, Air Mobility Command (Provisional), vol. 1, 15 January–31 May 1992, 1.
57. Ibid., 2.
58. Ibid.
59. Ibid., 3.
60. Kross, "Air Mobility Symposium Address," 260.
61. Hazdra, *Air Mobility*, 61–62.
62. Ibid., 61.
63. Ibid., 66.
64. Hutcheson, *Air Mobility*, 102.
65. Ibid., 103.
66. Under the EAF concept, the Air Force relies on "regularly scheduled rotations of [10] Air Expeditionary Forces (AEF)." Ibid., 45. The AEFs each have a cross section of weapon systems that accomplishes regular missions and is tailored to respond to crisis situations.
67. Quoted in ibid.
68. Ibid., 47.
69. Ibid., 61.

70. O'Hanlon, Rice, and Steinberg, "New Security Strategy and Preemption," 2.
71. Ibid., 3.
72. Ibid., 4.
73. See *National Military Strategy of the United States*, 2004.
74. Ibid., 7.
75. *Quadrennial Defense Review Report*, 53.
76. Air Force Doctrine Document (AFDD) 2-6, *Air Mobility Operations*, 1.
77. Ibid., 31.
78. Ibid., 41.
79. Quoted in ibid., 43.
80. Ibid., 34.
81. Hebert, "Air Mobility's Never-Ending Surge," 49.
82. Ibid. The Berlin airlift totaled 1.78 million tons of cargo from 1948 to 1949; airlift operations in Afghanistan and Iraq totaled 1.86 million tons of cargo in September 2006.
83. Hutcheson, *Air Mobility*, 129.
84. Air Mobility Command, *2006 Air Mobility Master Plan*, i.
85. Cassidy, transcript of interview, 75.

Chapter 3

The Rise of Mobility Generals

I have traveled around the world and talked to people in different countries. I can tell you that when those big "T" tail aircraft land, with the American flag on the tail, they not only represent America—they are America.

—Gen Ronald R. Fogleman

Geopolitical changes in the late twentieth and early twenty-first century caused a significant shift in US policy, which fueled major changes in the role and importance of air-mobility forces in the execution of national security strategy. The president and secretary of defense based the post–Cold War national security strategy on the "ability to rapidly project decisive combat power to any corner of the globe for a variety of reasons: economic interdependencies, military commitments, societal and ethnic concerns, or moral obligations."[1] As a result of this change in strategy, the United States engaged in a myriad of complex operations around the world that led the Air Force to become more expeditionary. In the process, air mobility often became more than a force enabler or a support element of the nation's strategy of containment during the Cold War. Today, air mobility frequently takes center stage and is absolutely essential to the success of the US policy of engagement around the world. According to Gen Walter Kross, former AMC commander, without AMC's first-in, last-out capabilities, "there is no national military strategy. Figure it out. Doesn't exist. Can't get there. Cannot be done. That's how important Air Mobility Command is. That's how important global air mobility is to our nation."[2] As the number and types of deployments increased dramatically through the mid-1990s, senior Air Force leaders recognized an increased need for officers with air-mobility expertise.[3]

So did officials in AMC. In the 1990s, they made a conscious decision not only to continue developing experts in air-mobility operations but also to expand the leadership-development program they inherited from their predecessors in MAC. These

AMC leaders took deliberate steps to broaden the command's outlook and develop senior leaders who were air-mobility experts and who understood the Defense Transportation System (DTS), broader Air Force policy, and national security issues. As a result, air-mobility leaders learned how to operate effectively across the full spectrum of military operations as well as in a wide variety of organizations throughout the defense establishment. Therefore, when the Air Force called for more general officers in the post–Cold War environment who had experience in airlift and/or air-refueling operations, AMC was prepared to offer a robust cadre of officers who quickly stepped up to lead complex mobility operations and who also could fill a variety of positions in the national security establishment that mobility officers had not traditionally held.

This chapter examines the rise of mobility generals in the post–Cold War era by first reviewing the unique mission expertise and competencies that air-mobility officers provide the nation. It then discusses organizational and cultural changes in AMC that enable the command to meet the needs of the war fighter more effectively. Finally, this section describes how AMC foreshadowed the Air Force's deliberate efforts to develop officers and explains the continuing effectiveness of the command's force-development program.

A Review of What Air-Mobility Experts Bring to the Fight

They [air mobility forces] must be at the planning table and involved in every aspect of military campaigning. If we do not properly account for air mobility, all strategy is doomed to fail and all planning is for naught.

—Brig Gen Chuck Wald
USAF Director of Strategic Planning, 1998

The essence of flexibility is in the mind of the commander; the substance of flexibility is in logistics.

—Rear Adm Henry Eccles, USN

Since the end of the Cold War, air-mobility crews have been continually on the move, participating in operations across the full spectrum of operations. In the opening stages of a conflict or humanitarian operation, air-mobility officers are frequently the first military members on the scene, and they are usually the last ones to leave after the crisis has subsided.[4] "More often than not, AMC has the lead," carrying "the nation's flag and its influence around the world," according to Gen Hansford T. Johnson, former commander of USTRANSCOM and MAC/AMC. "It's a very solemn responsibility."[5] Often operating autonomously in a high-threat environment, air-mobility aircrews learn early in their careers how to think on their feet, solve complex problems in foreign countries, and make decisions that can have far-reaching strategic effects. As a result, airlifters and air refuelers today not only bring valuable mission-related expertise to the fight but also embody a distinctive worldview and modus operandi that are combat tested, flexible, global, and at the same time realistic. This section discusses the mission expertise as well as the unique perspective that air-mobility officers contribute to the defense community.

US air-mobility forces are critical to the security of the United States, according to Gen T. Michael Moseley, Air Force chief of staff, because they provide "a very singular form of airpower: the ability to rapidly position and sustain forces at places and times of our choosing."[6] Although "other forms of American military power have some degree of inherent mobility, the scale of flexibility and responsiveness of the Air Force's air-mobility forces is singular in the history of world conflict."[7] In fact, no other country in the world has an air-mobility system like that of the United States. This system provides a capability vital to the nation's ability to protect the US homeland against external attacks; deter, coerce, and defeat adversaries in "critical regions of Northeast Asia, East Asian Littoral, Middle East/Southwest Asia, and Europe"; and respond quickly to any humanitarian crisis around the world.[8]

The success of the air-mobility mission is directly dependent on the skills and competencies of a professional cadre of air-mobility officers, who typically develop one of two primary areas of mission expertise—airlift and air refueling. In addition to that expertise, the changing nature of the post–Cold War environment and the "anti-access and anti-denial strategies" of US adversaries highlight the importance of two other emerging air-mobility missions: opening air bases in forward operating areas and evacuating injured or mortally wounded personnel from the battlefield.[9] Although these two missions have always represented air-mobility capabilities, they have recently increased in importance in the post–Cold War era.

Airlift, one of the Air Force's air and space power functions, is defined as the "ability to transport personnel (including casualties) and material through the air."[10] This mundane definition obscures the full range of airlift operations and the impact that those missions have on national security. "There are four basic airlift operations: Passenger and cargo movement including operational support airlift, combat employment and sustainment, aeromedical evacuation, and special operations support."[11] In general, passenger airlift includes transporting Defense Department and other government personnel as well as supporting unit rotations and deployments.[12] It also includes special missions to transport the nation's most senior officials around the world, together with operational-support missions dedicated to supporting MAJCOMs or other service components.[13] Cargo movement, on the other hand, includes the airlift of hazardous and nonhazardous material as well as bulk, oversized, and outsized supplies and equipment that "cannot wait for surface transportation."[14]

Besides airlifting passengers and cargo, air-mobility forces are responsible for combat employment and sustainment operations. These dangerous missions involve both the insertion of combat forces directly into combat and their resupply during hostilities. These operations, which range from noncombatant evacuations to "large scale air assault/air drop missions that may lead to base opening and force lodgment" require detailed planning as well as flexibility during the execution phase.[15] Although these types of missions account for only a small percentage of the total number of airlift sorties in an operation, they have far-reaching "importance and effectiveness."[16] One of the most impressive examples of this type of airlift mission occurred in late 2001 during Enduring Freedom. Mobility pilots flying C-17s and C-130s using night vision goggles supported Operation Swift Freedom, which involved "the US Marine seizure of [Camp

Rhino], a forward operating base in Southern Afghanistan."[17] Over the course of eight days and under the threat of surface-to-air missiles as well as antiaircraft and small-arms fire, mobility forces airlifted 481 troops, off-loaded 1,450 tons of supplies, and successfully executed "the deepest combat insertion in the 227-year history of the US Marine Corps."[18]

The third type of airlift operation, the aeromedical-evacuation mission, is more critical today than in the past due to the "highly lethal environment of today's battlefield and the reduced theater medical footprint" overseas.[19] With the addition of specially trained personnel, most mobility aircraft can fly this mission, which provides lifesaving in-flight medical support and transports casualties to more robust medical facilities.[20] Gen John W. Handy, former AMC commander, explained that during operations in Iraq, "without missing a beat for every patient in our care, we provided incredible medical capability on the ground up close to the battle, all the way through the [aeromedical-evacuation] system, to safe and secure hospitals for continued treatment. It's a remarkable story that continues today."[21]

The last type of airlift operation involves supporting special operations forces (SOF). Specially trained mobility-airlift aircrews usually conduct these operations in a hostile environment and are often part of a large, joint effort.[22] These missions require extensive planning and coordination between SOF units and conventional-airlift organizations. Recent operations in Iraq and Afghanistan reveal the increased use of airlift in these types of operations, and there is every indication that this trend will continue in the future.

In addition to airlift operations, air-mobility officers also provide the president and secretary of defense with air-refueling expertise—another Air Force function. Air refueling involves the "passing of fuel from an airborne tanker aircraft to a receiver aircraft. . . . [It] significantly expands the force options available to a commander by increasing the range, payload, persistence, and flexibility of other aircraft."[23] Throughout most of the Cold War, air-refueling planes sat alert, waiting to support a nuclear strike against the Soviet Union. Since the collapse of the USSR, however, the air-refueling community has been on the road nonstop. Applicable across the full spectrum of military operations, air refueling increases the effectiveness of airpower at the tactical, operational, and strategic levels of war.[24] This is especially true today. "Both Afghanistan and Iraq were air-mobility wars," according to General Handy. "Every single flight into these areas of operation needed some kind of air refueling—fighters, bombers, lifters and even other tankers needed air refueling. Navy carrier-based fighters needed dramatic air refueling to get them the 'legs' they needed."[25] AMC's air-refueling capabilities once again proved invaluable for the nation during that conflict by enabling the United States to first "defeat the tyranny of distance" before ultimately defeating the Taliban.[26]

Air-refueling assets support six primary operations: nuclear operations, global strike, air bridge, aircraft deployment, theater, and special operations. In terms of supporting nuclear operations, air-refueling experts continue training to refuel the nuclear-equipped bomber force, which provides the United States a viable nuclear-deterrent option against potential adversaries. Air-refueling assets are also critical to the success of long-range global-strike missions, where they "are employed to give strike platforms the ability to reach any target globally without relying on intermediate basing locations."[27] By increasing the range of global-strike aircraft, such as the B-1, B-2, and B-52, air-refueling planes enable operations to originate in the United States or from locations far from hostilities.

Military planners also employ air-refueling aircraft in support of air-bridge operations. "An air bridge creates an air line of communication linking" the United States and a theater of operations.[28] Similar to global-strike missions, air refueling enables airlift assets to originate in the United States and fly directly to the combat zone or any other desired location. An air bridge reduces en route refueling and maintenance on the ground and "increases the efficiency and effectiveness of airlift operations by making possible the direct delivery of personnel and material."[29] The synergy of air refueling and airlift, therefore, makes the factory-to-foxhole concept a reality. Just as they support an air bridge, so do air-refueling assets support aircraft deployment, which increases the range of combat and combat-support aircraft deploying overseas for contingencies, rotations, exercises, or logistics purposes.[30] These operations, often referred to as Coronets, are distinct from air bridges because they usually involve fighter aircraft and require more extensive planning and coordination.

In addition to supporting aircraft deploying overseas, air-refueling assets provide extensive support directly to aircraft in the theater of operations. US commanders have relied on tankers and the expertise of tanker planners in every conflict in the post–Cold War era. Quite simply, air refueling can make or break theater operations, and it nearly did in Operation Allied Force. The success of that operation depended totally on US air-refueling capability. During the 78-day war over Kosovo, 175 tankers flew 5,000 sorties and off-loaded 250 million pounds of fuel to enable 24,000 combat and combat-support sorties.[31] "Tankers were at the heart of the fight," according to Lt Gen William Begert, vice-commander of Headquarters USAFE during Allied Force.[32] "Tankers provided the backbone of the air campaign and the lifeblood of an operation that would have been impossible without air refueling."[33] As Kosovo and recent operations in Afghanistan and Iraq proved, air refueling is especially important in the early stages of a conflict, when major combat operations are the main priority for air component commanders. Likewise, air refueling is also critical to success during later stages of an operation because it enables combat-patrol and combat-support aircraft to remain on station for longer periods of time and thereby provide US presence during stability operations. Besides theater support, air-refueling assets provide special-operations support. Specially trained aircrews, in coordination with special-operations personnel, plan and execute SOF missions in support of the president and secretary of defense or a theater commander's objectives.

Air-mobility officers also provide combat support on the ground. Because mobility aircraft are often the first to arrive at the scene of a crisis or humanitarian disaster, AMC personnel have become experts in expanding the en route global-mobility structure and in opening as well as supporting airfields in austere locations. This area of expertise is especially relevant today because of the post–Cold War pullback from overseas bases.[34] Mobility personnel fill this vital niche by providing robust aerial-port and maintenance support as well as by establishing critical command and control (C2) networks, which help provide seamless intertheater and intratheater airlift and in-transit visibility of all cargo and equipment. In performing this mission in support of the Air Force, other services, or coalition partners, mobility personnel work directly with host-nation officials, or, following a base seizure, they may work autonomously without the support of the local community.[35] This was the case during Enduring Freedom, when air-mobility operators opened Mazar e-Sharif, one of the first airfields seized from the Taliban in Afghanistan. After members of the air-mobility contingency-response team arrived on the scene, "they found a war-torn area devoid of water, plumbing, electricity, communications, and only a primitive transportation infrastructure."[36] The team, however, quickly had the airfield operational and transformed it into a transportation center for follow-on American and coalition forces as well as commercial carriers and international aid organizations. Air-mobility experts performed impressively under extremely hostile conditions and were soon able to establish Mazar e-Sharif as "an important strategic hub for US and coalition forces in the Global War on Terrorism."[37]

Opening the air base at Mazar e-Sharif is just one of many recent examples of the employment of air-mobility expertise in combat. Today, combat experience and a combat mind-set are prevalent throughout the air-mobility community. According to Maj Gen Kip Self, former commander of the 314th Airlift Wing, the current generation is the most combat-tested group of air-mobility officers since Vietnam.[38] In fact, statistics reveal that air-mobility aircraft are currently the most heavily tasked Air Force weapon systems in the Middle East.[39] A combat mind-set helps bring mobility forces and the CAF closer together—when combat is indeed the order of the day.

The mobility community's perspective, however, is unique in that air-mobility experts also regularly employ their skills in peacetime and in peacekeeping and humanitarian-response operations, which are considered high threat but do not qualify as major combat. Because air mobility has played such an important role in these types of operations over the past 15 years, it is a continuous challenge for air-mobility officers "to meet peacetime demand and to maintain wartime readiness."[40] Mobility officers are able to meet the challenge and routinely shift "between the worlds of logistics and combat" and employ their skills across the full spectrum of operations because they recognize the importance of maintaining a flexible attitude.[41]

It is a rare occurrence today to read an air-mobility article that does not champion the flexibility of "T-tail" aircrews. For example, in 2006 a standard C-17 airlift mission in Iraq evolved into a lifesaving aeromedical evacuation for a US marine. On 29 September, a C-17 aircrew originally planned to fly an Iraqi Freedom mission from Balad AB to Al Udeid AB. That night, however, LCpl Justin Ping suffered severe battlefield injuries and needed to be evacuated from Balad to Brooke Army Medical Center in San Antonio, Texas. The C-17 was "re-tasked for the duty, and a critical care air transport team was assembled. Enroute tankers from Mildenhall AB and the New Hampshire Air National Guard met the C-17 for multiple air refuelings, enabling the medical team to admit Justin into intensive care just 15 hours after he left Balad, ultimately saving the brave Marine's life."[42]

Likewise, the air-mobility mission demands that its officers think globally. Lt Col Glen R. Downing describes this global mind-set as "the strongest and most distinct element of the air-mobility culture."[43] General Self explains that air-mobility officers develop this perspective early in their careers because they are on their own, out in the world facing challenges that force them to think on their feet and make decisions as young aircraft commanders.[44] In fact, General Kross, former fighter pilot and AMC commander, considered this aspect of the air-mobility mission one of the most important and rewarding of his career.[45] While his peers in the CAF undoubtedly faced their own challenges, the amount of autonomy and responsibility given to General Kross early in his career stemmed from the global nature of the mobility mission.[46] Gen Ronald R. Fogleman, former AMC commander and Air Force chief of staff, concurred as he described how young commanders of air-mobility aircraft flying in remote regions like Africa have to make decisions on their own. As a fighter pilot, he never had to do anything like that because there was always a C2 element making those decisions for him.[47]

Whether airlifting cargo or patients, off-loading fuel, or opening up air bases in peacetime or during a crisis, mobility operators bring a skill set and combat-tested, global worldview that is instrumental to the success of US security strategy in the post–Cold War era.

Organizational Changes and the Cultural Development of Air Mobility Command

Get there firstest with the mostest.
—Gen Nathan Bedford Forrest

The geopolitical changes that increased the demand for air-mobility expertise in the post–Cold War years coincided with significant organizational and cultural changes within the air-mobility community. These changes occurred because senior leaders realized that the air-mobility structure and culture based on a Cold War worldview were outdated. These organizational and cultural changes are important to delineate because in many ways they directly contributed to the rise of air-mobility generals within the Air Force and the defense community. If internal organization and the culture shifts had not kept pace with geopolitical changes, AMC leaders might not have been able to meet the increasing demand for air-mobility resources. Consequently, air-mobility generals may have become irrelevant or replaced by leaders from the CAF and never given the chance to assume more senior roles within the national security establishment. This section reviews the major organizational and cultural changes that took place within AMC and the transportation community in recent years and relates them to the rise of mobility generals in the post–Cold War era.

The first major organizational change affecting mobility generals in the post–Cold War era occurred before the collapse of the Soviet Union. Due to the increasingly important role that transportation played in the execution of national security strategy in the late twentieth century, the Defense Department established USTRANSCOM in 1987. Despite initial growing pains, it soon came of age during Desert Shield and Desert Storm, due in large part to the leadership of Gen Hansford Johnson, commander of USTRANSCOM, MAC, and, later, AMC. According to General Fogleman, "It was the manner in which General Johnson conducted himself and the credibility he gained in Desert Shield/Desert Storm that convinced people this new organization called TRANSCOM has a great future."[48] Further, General Fogleman believed it was USTRANSCOM's performance in the war that led Secretary of Defense Richard Cheney in 1992 to designate it the nation's single manager of all defense-transportation resources in both peacetime and wartime.[49] In addition, USTRANSCOM gained greater responsibilities when it became the Defense Department's distribution process owner (DPO) in 2003.[50]

In terms of the rise of mobility generals, the creation of USTRANSCOM was significant for several reasons. First, because it was one of the unified combatant commands, the status of transportation—and thereby air mobility—rose to a new level within the defense community.[51] Prior to the creation of USTRANSCOM, the transportation community lacked coherent policy and leadership. "No one understands logistics in the Department of Defense [DOD]," General Handy explained, because of the "vacuum of knowledge in Washington."[52] With the creation of USTRANSCOM, however, AMC leaders successfully filled this void. Second, from 1987 until 2005, the commander of USTRANSCOM was also the AMC commander.[53] In this dual-hatted position, air-mobility generals had the opportunity to gain valuable experience leading a complex joint organization and in so doing established credibility with the president and secretary of defense, Congress, and other senior leaders in the defense environment following the Goldwater-Nichols Department of Defense Reorganization Act of 1986. The first USTRANSCOM commander, Gen Duane H. Cassidy, remarked that as a unified commander "you carry considerably more weight. You are much more accepted into 'the club.'. . . You create a unified command to get it out from underneath the Services to work directly for the Chairman and the Secretary of Defense, so the tasking and communication lines can be more clear, direct, faster."[54] Third, since its creation, USTRANSCOM has been responsible for developing cutting-edge C2 systems such as the Global Transportation Network, a network of networks that serves as the foundation for today's efficient and effective DTS.[55] Without this system, the DTS would not be as flexible and responsive, and air-mobility generals would not be nearly as successful in meeting the needs of war fighters and other customers.

Another major organizational change that facilitated the rise of mobility generals was the creation of AMC in 1992. Soon after the command stood up, AMC leaders took deliberate steps to complete the consolidation of airlift and tanker operations. Previously, airlift assets were in the Twenty-first and Twenty-second Air Forces, and tanker units were in Fifteenth Air Force. AMC disestablished the Twenty-second and placed both assets in the remaining two numbered air forces. These organizational changes and the merging of most of the airlift and tanker assets into one command and two air forces established a new era and symbolized a break from the past, which facilitated new ways of thinking about air mobility. AMC's first commander, General Johnson, went so far as to change the name of command-unique activities from *Volant*, meaning *flying*, to *Phoenix*, which referred to "the legendary bird that consumed itself by fire after 500 years and rose renewed from its ashes."[56] In addition, General Johnson changed the call sign of the command's aircraft from MAC to REACH, which better suited the new mission.[57] He also took down pictures of former MAC commanders to make sure he thoroughly "disestablished MAC and established Air Mobility Command."[58]

This break from the past invigorated mobility experts and allowed them to build the command essentially from the ground up in order to better serve the nation and meet the needs of its customers. The consolidation of airlift and tanker resources into one command created more synergy and enabled the more efficient use of limited airlift and air-refueling assets. Likewise, the reorganization placed 50 percent of the nation's air-mobility capability in the Reserve forces, compelling AMC leaders to develop close partnerships with their Reserve counterparts during peacetime. The provisional AMC commander, General Kross, established the Total Force mentality from the start by ensuring that the reserves became fully involved in the day-to-day decision activities of the command up through full mobilization.[59] This mentality paid fortuitous dividends for AMC and air-mobility generals down the road because it assured smoother mobility operations and a seamless transition when the nation called on mobility air forces to respond to contingencies. As Gen Michael Ryan observed, "It is the personal relationship in combat upon which our total force lays it foundation."[60]

As airlift and air refueling merged into one command, and as mobility officers began developing close partnerships with their Reserve counterparts, AMC leaders recognized the need to improve the C2 of their forces. This realization constituted the third major organizational change in AMC and led to the creation of the tanker airlift control center (TACC) in 1992. Comprised of 10 divisions and approximately 900 people, the TACC streamlined processes previously divided between two numbered air forces and became the single point of contact for those commands using AMC assets. As a result, air-mobility experts gained a more global view of the world. Today, the TACC is the epicenter of AMC and "combines airlift, air-refueling, and mobility-support assets into an integrated team that performs its wartime mission every day and expands as necessary to meet contingency requirements."[61] On a day-to-day basis, it "tasks units to schedule, task, manage, coordinate, control, and execute AMC missions and requirements."[62] More centralized control of limited air-mobility assets means improved flexibility and responsiveness throughout the command. For example, because TACC controllers have the authority and capability to retask mobility aircraft while they are airborne, AMC can respond quickly to changing situations or emerging crises.[63] In addition, as the hub of all air-mobility operations, the TACC is currently the longest-standing air and space operations center in the Air Force. By creating a robust, state-of-the-art C2 capability and by developing and promoting leaders who grew up and understood how to operate effectively in complex and changing environments, AMC and its generals were out in front of the rest of the Air Force.

The fourth major organizational change affecting the development of air-mobility leaders was the activation of the Air Mobility Warfare Center in 1994. This organization, recently renamed the United States Air Force Expeditionary Center, serves as AMC's "single focal point for advanced education, training, and testing."[64] Today, the center graduates almost 9,000 students a year, and its curriculum has expanded to more than 60 in-residence courses and 12 accredited Web-based courses.[65] One of the center's primary courses, Eagle Flag, prepares air-mobility personnel for combat, according to General Handy, by creating a "Red Flag–like environment" for expeditionary combat-support personnel.[66] The center consists of a Resource Directorate, an Air Mobility Battlelab, a Mobility Operations School, an Expeditionary Operations School, and, until recently, a Mobility Weapons School.[67] Creation of the warfare center was a major step forward in AMC maturation and air-mobility leadership development because it helped establish a warrior mentality and combat focus previously missing in the command. Today, the Air Force recognizes the unit as a center of excellence whose mission is to "teach warfighting to the Airmen of AMC" and whose commanders continue to rise to positions of greater importance within the defense community.[68]

Another significant change that affected the development of senior air-mobility leaders was the creation of the concept of the air and space expeditionary force (AEF). As discussed in the previous chapter, the Air Force took steps in 1997 to reorganize and become more expeditionary. Changes in the geopolitical environment and a reduction in overseas bases drove these organizational changes. Air mobility proved critical to the ongoing success of the AEF because it was "essential to seizing the initiative rapidly, containing conflict, and resolving the situation on terms favorable to the United States."[69] The implementation of the AEF concept proved an important step in the development of air-mobility generals because, like the creation of USTRANSCOM, it raised the status and further highlighted the importance of air mobility within the defense community. Air-mobility assets, according to General Kross, played *the* critical early role in the AEF because "when the miscreants see that we are coming, we being America, that is when they pay up their insurance. That is when they go underground. It is the *coming* that modifies behavior" (emphasis in original).[70] The AEF concept also helped establish closer relationships between CAF leaders and mobility generals because the planning process facilitated communication between the commands. Better communication not only leads to increased trust between the commands but also enables mobility generals to better meet the needs of their primary AEF customers, in this case, the CAF and the regional combatant commanders.

One of the most recent organizational changes to influence the rise of air-mobility generals has been the dissolution of AMC's two numbered air forces (the Fifteenth and Twenty-first) and the creation of Eighteenth Air Force and the 15th and 21st

Expeditionary Mobility Task Forces (EMTF) in 2003. The restructuring of the command reflected both the continuing need for air mobility to become more efficient and effective in the post–Cold War years and the continued evolution of AMC toward becoming a more combat-oriented organization. Creation of the EMTFs resulted from geopolitical changes that highlighted the increased need for AMC experts to be able to expand the en route global-mobility structure as well as open and sustain airfields in austere locations around the world. AMC designed the two EMTFs to accomplish these tasks and better meet war fighters' needs by presenting "light, lean, and agile response forces" to the six combatant commanders.[71]

The heart of the EMTF is a fixed network of overseas bases that "provide[s] en route support to air and space forces" on a regular basis and that can quickly expand within 12 hours of notification during a crisis situation.[72] "This capability gives warfighting commands the flexibility to place expeditionary forces according to need . . . and provides a foundation of rapid projection and sustainment of US military might."[73] Likewise, although the EMTFs focus on supporting the war fighter, they are also critical to the success of humanitarian operations. Personnel from the contingency response groups in the EMTFs have supported relief efforts after Hurricane Katrina, Hurricane Rita, the noncombatant evacuation of citizens from Lebanon in 2006, and the previously mentioned devastating earthquake in Pakistan in 2005.[74] In each situation, the EMTF increased the responsiveness of air mobility and better met the needs of the customer.

Like the effect of the creation of the EMTFs, Eighteenth Air Force also improved air mobility's effectiveness by streamlining and consolidating processes under a single command. During the Cold War, MAC divided the world between east and west, delegating the execution of eastbound missions to Twenty-first Air Force and westbound missions to Fifteenth Air Force. Because of AMC's global worldview and the TACC's success at exercising centralized C2, this organizational structure no longer made sense. General Handy decided in 2003 that the two numbered air forces only added a layer of bureaucracy to the organization.[75] Subsequently, he disbanded the two units, created a single numbered air force at Scott AFB, Illinois, and had the TACC report directly to Eighteenth Air Force instead of the

AMC commander. By consolidating the numbered air forces, AMC lost two major-general billets but maintained two one-star billets in the EMTFs and gained a three-star billet by establishing the Eighteenth.[76] Ultimately, these major organizational changes were worth the effort, having the desired effect of streamlining the command and increasing the efficiency of AMC and the effectiveness of air-mobility generals.

The major organizational changes in the mobility community occurred alongside, and in many ways helped facilitate, the development of a new culture within the post–Cold War mobility community. This development was important because it not only stimulated new ways of thinking about air-mobility operations but also affected how the defense community perceived AMC and its leaders. This was important to General Fogleman, who subsequently became one of the strongest advocates of developing a new mobility culture and mind-set.[77] This is interesting because he was not originally an air-mobility operator but a fighter pilot. He assumed command of the mobility air forces soon after the formation of AMC in 1992. Although many mobility operators scoffed at the idea of an outsider taking over the command, General Fogleman's fresh perspective benefited the command in the long term because he had no allegiance to legacy systems and/or old ways of doing business.[78] In addition, he viewed the command from the perspective of its primary war-fighting customers, and he could help shape it to meet their needs. This further facilitated the development of a new culture and a new generation of mobility leaders.

From the start, General Fogleman realized how different AMC would be from MAC and SAC. Given Pres. George H. W. Bush's planned reduction of forces overseas, General Fogleman was acutely aware of the critical role that air mobility and USTRANSCOM would play in the post–Cold War era—even before he assumed command.[79] "The tanker force, historically tied to nuclear alert, would now be available for day-to-day conventional tasking. That reality, combined with the historic strategic airlift force and its air-refueling capability, gave us [AMC] a whole new concept of strategic mobility to support the new, larger Air Force mosaic of Global Reach/Global Power."[80] Armed with this knowledge, General Fogleman focused on creating a professional mobility culture and instilling a warrior spirit in the command, which complemented the important role that air mobility now played in national security.[81]

He faced several challenges, one of which was breaking down the "airlifter and aerial refueler as second-class citizens" syndrome.[82] He believed that this perception no longer mattered because the nation now "put a premium" on air mobility, which was "the keystone to deterrence, the bedrock of national strategy."[83] According to General Fogleman, "That wasn't just rhetoric. It was fact." Consequently, if the air-mobility community wished to be the center of national security strategy, he pointed out, the command should look and act the part.[84]

Combining two very different communities—air refuelers and airlifters—into a single command presented another major challenge for General Fogleman. The tanker community consisted of professional SAC warriors who spent most of their careers in garrison, on alert, and laser focused on supporting a nuclear strike against the Soviets. Their mission led to a more rigid, limited view of the world and to very different traditions and operating procedures, compared to the mission of their MAC counterparts. Members of the tanker community ultimately experienced more culture shock than the airlifters in the post–Cold War environment because they had to develop an expeditionary mind-set. Lt Gen Christopher Kelly, AMC vice-commander, recalled the challenges of changing the mind-set of tanker aircrews who grew up in SAC only to wake up one morning and find themselves in AMC. As commander of a tanker operations group in the early days of AMC, after one of his squadron-operations officers burst into his office complaining about the number of taskings and deployments, General Kelly asked him to look down and read the words on the AMC patch on his flight suit. "Air *Mobility* Command," the general said, "means we don't do it here!"[85]

General Fogleman foresaw this type of challenge and began the task of combining two very different communities by first selecting an air-refueling pilot, Lt Gen John E. Jackson Jr., as his vice-commander. Next, he instituted a cross-flow program whereby air-refueling operators transferred at both the junior and senior levels to airlift units and vice versa. He also stood up the Air Mobility Warfare Center to educate the tanker and airlift communities about the total-mobility system and instituted the Advanced Study of Air Mobility Master's Program—one of the resident education programs at the center. In addition, he advocated the increased use of KC-135 and KC-10 aircraft in an airlift role and "put tanker people into the forefront of deployments."[86]

General Fogleman also furthered the integration of tankers into the mobility culture when he persuaded the Airlift Association to change its name and charter. In the fall of 1992, he advised the organization's leadership that he would not support it unless it included the tanker community and changed its name to the Airlift/Tanker Association (A/TA).[87] He also prodded the organization to make the focus more on professional development and less on socialization. Today the association has grown into a national organization with over 8,000 members and is one of the most respected and professional groups of its kind. Half of the membership attends the A/TA annual convention and symposium each year, which brings together active duty, civilian, and retired members of the air-mobility community as well as industry representatives and senior Air Force and national defense leaders. "No other organization," according to General Cassidy, "connects the young people in the mobility business with senior people in the mobility business like A/TA."[88] The symposium includes four days of professional-development seminars focused on issues concerning air mobility and national security. In addition to professional development, the social aspect of the A/TA convention remains important because it provides a unique opportunity for people from across the command to network and establish relationships, which improves AMC's operations and strengthens the mobility culture.

Although the air-refueling community experienced most of the culture shock in the 1990s, airlifters also had to change.[89] General Fogleman believed that airlift crews had to become more professional and needed to improve their image as "trash haulers" or "bus drivers" who flew "big dumpy airplanes."[90] After taking command, he pledged to issue reprimands in the form of Article 15s to anyone who referred to himself as a trash hauler or who had his sleeves rolled up or a plastic spoon visible in the left-shoulder pocket of his flight suit.[91] General Fogleman quietly but very quickly assisted into retirement a general officer who made an inappropriate "plastic spoon" comment to him in an official conversation, which indicated that this officer could not let go of the stereotyped past.[92]

Besides improving the image of airlifters, General Fogleman ensured that they became more proficient in air-refueling operations. Not only did they cross-flow into the tanker community but also General Fogleman demanded that the maximum number of airlifters become qualified in air refueling.[93] Because of the reduced number of contingency operations and the robust en route system during the Cold War, no strong need existed for airlifters to develop this skill. However, in Fogleman's view, that was no longer true. Airlifters qualified to do air refueling created increased flexibility within the system and helped foster a culture and community of operators who better understood both the airlift and air-refueling missions.

There were additional challenges within the airlift community. During the Cold War, two subcultures had developed—strategic airlift and tactical airlift, affectionately known as Big MAC and Little MAC, respectively. This division, caused by different missions, dated to the creation of MAC in the 1960s and "the initial transfer of tactical airlift forces from TAC to MAC in the 1970s."[94] For the next 20 years, an underlying tension existed between strategic airlifters, who controlled MAC and "focus[ed] on the efficiencies" of centralizing C2 at MAC headquarters, and the tactical airlifters, who "focus[ed] on the effectiveness" of centralizing C2 at the theater level.[95] These differences were alive and well at the time AMC stood up in 1992. As a result, tactical as well as operational-support airlift became orphans once again and shifted to the CAF in ACC.[96]

In 1997, however, the C-130s and C-21s transferred back to the mobility community. This latest transfer of tactical and operational-support airlift once again gave AMC unity of command of most fixed-wing mobility assets.[97] General Kross facilitated their reintegration into the command by recognizing all of their accomplishments in ACC, such as defensive-system testing and combat-capability refinement.[98] More importantly, however, he gave them fiscal priority and approved the C-130 modernization program, which, according to General Kross, would not "have happened if they had remained in Air Combat Command."[99] Although differences still exist in the airlift subcultures, the broader community is more integrated today than in the past. Traditional strategic-airlift aircraft are performing more direct-delivery missions to the theater, and the C-17, which became operational in the 1990s, has "a foot in both the strategic and tactical worlds."[100] Over time, the blurring of the lines between strategic and tactical airlift led AMC to stop distinguishing between strategic and tactical aircraft, instead referring to airlift as either intertheater or intratheater.[101] This change in nomenclature and the fact that the past two AMC commanders and the present USTRANSCOM commander are C-130 pilots further indicate that AMC is moving toward a seamless mobility culture.

This section highlighted the major organizational and cultural changes within the air-mobility community over the past 20 years. What began as a loosely aligned federation of airlifters and air refuelers in the early 1990s is now a combat-tested air-mobility community that managed to let go of many outdated paradigms and adjust to the new realities of the post–Cold War era.[102] In the process of integrating airlift and air-refueling operations and establishing an air-mobility culture, the community became more efficient and effective—and ultimately more responsive to the wider world. Although AMC has come a long way organizationally and culturally since its inception, work still remains—a fact that may further affect the rise of mobility generals in the future. The next chapter addresses several of those issues. At this point in the discussion, it is important to recognize that the organizational and cultural changes to date facilitated the rise of air-mobility generals in the post–Cold War era by helping to "create a light, lean, lethal, well-organized organization postured for the war fight, leading the way for the Air Force."[103]

Development of Air-Mobility General Officers

Amateurs talk about tactics, but professionals study logistics.

—Gen Robert H. Barrow
Commandant of the Marine Corps, 1980

While the air-mobility community changed to meet the demands of a shifting world, the command championed innovative and effective leadership-development programs. According to General Handy, the air-mobility community has always been proactive about identifying and developing its future leaders early in their careers.[104] Beginning in the 1970s, MAC established a leadership program called Volant Spotlight, designed to bring young captains to air-mobility headquarters in order to expose them to the inner workings of the staff at an early point in their careers. Volant Spotlight evolved over the years, eventually becoming a yearlong internship and the only program of its type at the MAJCOM level.[105] This program proved successful in identifying several officers who are senior air-mobility leaders today. The success of Volant Spotlight set the stage for the future, enabling AMC to take the program to the next level and thereby lead the Air Force in instituting a culture of deliberate leadership and force development. This section describes several aspects of AMC's leadership-development program and explains its part in the rise of air mobility and air-mobility generals in the post–Cold War era.

AMC's leadership-development program grew exponentially under the guidance and vision of General Fogleman. In a meeting with his field commanders soon after he assumed command in 1992, he acknowledged that a non-air-mobility officer became the AMC commander because "there was a void" of air-mobility three-star generals who were ready to become full generals at that time.[106] It was not a matter of ability or capacity to do the job but a lack of deliberate force development that led to a fighter pilot's leading AMC. Force development consequently became the cornerstone of his vision for the command.[107] He explained that he made a pact to "begin working immediately to grow the future leadership of this command, so that it would never again have an outsider at its helm."[108]

The philosophy behind deliberate force development eschews an "unstructured and happenstance approach" toward the education and training of air-mobility leaders.[109] Rather, General Fogleman favored a structured program that identified and developed leaders with the right mix of competencies and experience required to lead in the twenty-first century.[110] The goal, importantly, was not simply to produce more air-mobility generals but to produce better leaders for the Air Force and the nation.[111] AMC began institutionalizing the concept of deliberate force development soon after General Fogleman took command. In this regard, he and AMC were out in front of the Air Force, which did not begin deliberate force development until 2000.[112] The AMC program began in the Directorate of Personnel, now known as the A1 Directorate of Manpower and Personnel, and was the only MAJCOM-level program of its kind. General Fogleman instituted a higher- and a lower-level component to this force development. At the higher level, AMC needed to proactively develop future generals who were generalists or individuals with broad knowledge and skills in several areas. This contrasted with conventional thinking in many of the other MAJCOMs.[113] Under General Fogleman's guidance, the command began to identify opportunities to broaden its best senior officers and place them in positions outside the air-mobility community, with an eye toward developing a future cadre of officers who understood not only air mobility but also the larger Air Force and Defense Department. Thereafter, the general and his successors fought hard to place air-mobility officers on staffs and in key jobs that were not typically air-mobility positions.[114] In order to increase the credibility of air-mobility officers, General Fogleman believed that AMC needed to push its best people forward, allowing the rest of the Defense Department to witness the level of talent within the community and inspiring other air-mobility officers to "up their game."[115]

One of the best examples of this type of higher-level force development occurred in the mid-1990s. The drawdown of forces after the Cold War, when the United States became involved in resolving the humanitarian crisis in Bosnia, resulted in a dearth of senior officers with air-mobility expertise in USAFE.[116] During Operation Deliberate Force, Lt Gen Michael E. Ryan, commander of Sixteenth Air Force, relied heavily on stateside air-mobility experts, especially General Begert, USTRANSCOM's director of operations and logistics. When General Ryan became the USAFE commander, he realized that he needed to put more air-mobility expertise back in the command and create a C2 network able to project mobility throughout the theater.[117] Based on the trust and confidence he had in General Begert and, importantly, the willingness of General Kross, the

THE RISE OF MOBILITY GENERALS

AMC commander, to push forward his best leaders, General Ryan selected General Begert to become the vice-commander of USAFE—a position traditionally held by a fighter pilot. In fact, this was the first time since Gen William H. Tunner served as the commander of USAFE in the 1950s that an air-mobility general above the rank of two stars served in Europe or any of the other overseas commands. This selection, therefore, amounted to quite "a significant thing" for the air-mobility community.[118]

During General Begert's tenure as vice-commander of USAFE, conflict broke out in Kosovo. Allied Force placed a high demand on air-refueling and intertheater-airlift assets, thereby giving General Begert the opportunity to play a direct role not only in mobility but also in the full breadth of Air Force combat operations.[119] Because of General Begert's leadership during the operation, in May 2001 Air Force Chief of Staff Ryan selected him to assume command of PACAF—another first for the air-mobility community. The traditionally fighter-centric Pacific theater received him well, according to General Begert, because by this time, he was not considered "a mobility guy" but a general officer with a mobility background who had credibility in other important aspects of Air Force business.[120]

This is not to say that his early career experiences flying C-141s and C-5s around the Pacific did not help him prepare for the job. On the contrary, they played a key role when he interviewed with Adm Dennis Blair, the commander of United States Pacific Command. During their first meeting, Admiral Blair expressed concern that General Begert's only assignment in the theater dated back to his tour as a forward air controller during the Vietnam War. After General Begert explained that as an airlifter he had significant experience flying in the Pacific, Admiral Blair "got it" and approved him for the position.[121] In his capacity as PACAF commander, however, General Begert also made sure to surround himself with experts in the theater who understood those parts of the Air Force that lay outside his area of expertise, such as fighters, intelligence, and space.[122] Consequently, General Begert demonstrated that, given the right opportunities and broadening experiences, a general officer who grew up in the air-mobility community could rise to the top of a combat-oriented organization.

Besides broadening air-mobility officers at the higher levels of the Air Force, AMC recognized the need to identify individuals who demonstrated leadership potential early in their careers and develop a program that gave them opportunities to grow. What began under General Fogleman's watch as an airlift-/tanker-pilot exchange program has grown into a robust Phoenix Horizon executive-development program, which charges an AMC-managed selection board to identify the best-qualified air-mobility officers for leadership development based on Air Force requirements.[123] The goal of this benchmark program is to "create a large pool of highly competitive mobility officers" by first *identifying* future air-mobility leaders assigned within and outside AMC, *tracking* them in a worldwide database through O-6 selection, and finally *placing* graduates of professional military education programs, squadron commanders, and other high-potential mobility officers in key joint, Office of the Secretary of Defense (OSD), and Air Staff positions.[124]

Four programs fall under the Phoenix Horizon umbrella: Phoenix Hawk, Phoenix Mobility, Phoenix Reach, and the Mobility Weapons Instructor Course (WIC). Similar to MAC's Volant Spotlight program, Phoenix Hawk is AMC's premier two-year intern program, which includes 11 rated and nonrated mobility officers, as well as two exchange officers from the space community, with four to eight years of service; these officers work one year in the TACC and one on the AMC staff.[125] Upon graduation, the rated officers cross-flow into another air-mobility aircraft, an experience that furthers the development of well-rounded mobility officers and the creation of a mobility culture across the command. Since its inception in 1994, the program has graduated 120 officers, three-fourths of whom are still on active duty. More than 80 percent of the Phoenix Hawk graduates are intermediate developmental education (IDE) selects, compared to approximately 25 percent in the entire Air Force. Likewise, 100 percent of the graduates were selected "in the zone" to major while 16 percent were selected "below the primary zone" (BPZ) to lieutenant colonel, which trumps fourfold the average 4 percent BPZ promotion rate throughout the Air Force.[126]

Phoenix Mobility is a relatively new program designed to educate mobility officers on the EMTF mission. Created in 2004, it fills "a critical need in mobility officer development" and includes eight rated officers with four to eight years of service for a tour of 30–36 months at one of AMC's two EMTFs.[127] Unlike participants in Phoenix Hawk, Phoenix Mobility officers continue to fly during their broadening tour—half of which occurs in the contingency-response group or global support squadron and the other half in the air-mobility operations squadron. However, like officers in the Phoenix Hawk program, those in Phoenix Mobility usually cross-flow at the completion of their internship. The resources and emphasis that AMC places on the Phoenix Mobility program indicate how much the command values the EMTF mission in the post-9/11 environment. It also reveals that by deliberately trying to build a cadre of officers who have the contingency-response mission as a core competency, the command continues to develop future mobility leaders who are experts in all aspects of air-mobility operations.

Phoenix Reach is another developmental program that "allows the best-qualified captains and majors to crossflow from any [air mobility] major weapon system to any other [air mobility] major weapon system."[128] Unlike the CAF community, which rarely retrains pilots in other major weapon systems, the mobility community avoids stovepiping officers by cross-flowing its future senior leaders so that they have experience in all aspects of the air-mobility mission. This is an expensive program for AMC to maintain, but it is indicative of the value the command places on broadening and deliberately developing its officers. Since 1994 AMC's Phoenix Reach has graduated 338 pilots and navigators, of whom 153 are IDE graduates/selects, for a 45 percent selection rate, and 54 BPZ officers, for a 16 percent selection rate, which again surpasses the Air Force–wide selection rate for both categories.

The final Phoenix Horizon program is the WIC, a graduate-level flying program that targets mobility pilots and navigators with nine years of service. To date, the WIC has graduated 290 officers who are experts in their mobility weapon systems and therefore highly valued by wing-level and combatant-commander staffs. Previously the WIC fell under the Air Mobility Weapons School, and AMC managed the selection process. Recently, however, the Air Force centralized all of the weapons schools under ACC and now picks individuals via a central selection board at the Air Force Personnel Center (AFPC) in San Antonio, Texas. Although the AFPC centrally selects WIC candidates, AMC continues to track them in its worldwide Phoenix Horizon database and develops them through the O-6 level.

AMC also deliberately identifies, tracks, and places its future leaders through its squadron-commander selection process, referred to as the Phoenix Eagle board. Squadron command, usually the first command experience for rated officers, is a significant indicator of leadership potential. Whom AMC selects for squadron command and how it selects them play a large role in the rise of air-mobility generals. AMC, therefore, conducts a rigorous screening process, which includes developing an Eighteenth Air Force game plan for placing the right individuals in the right command at the right time. Implementing the squadron-commander game plan is labor intensive and time consuming but effective because it allows AMC to develop well-rounded mobility leaders and forces the command to think through the second- and third-order effects of each placement decision. It also enables "many sets of eyes" to see the game plan, which helps ensure that the command is putting the most capable and competitive leaders in the right command positions.[129] The Phoenix Eagle board is unique to AMC because most of the functional and MAJCOM squadron-commander boards are centralized at AFPC today.[130] AMC prefers to continue conducting its own board at Scott AFB because it can play a more active role in developing its future leaders if it continues to maintain oversight of the board. Centralizing the board at AFPC is easier from a manpower perspective. However, removing AMC from the process would render the command's leaders less able to mentor individuals whom they are already tracking in the AMC database.[131]

AMC's efforts to develop leaders for the future have been effective. Although the first Phoenix Horizon graduates are just now becoming senior officers, higher IDE and BPZ selection rates are an indication of their potential to continue rising in the ranks as well as a measure of the program's success. AMC officers' BPZ selection rate to colonel also reflects the effectiveness of the command's program for deliberate force development. In every year but one from 1997 to 2006, AMC's rate was 1 percent higher than that of both the Air Force and the MAJ-

COMs—a fact of some significance because BPZ selection is an unofficial prerequisite for becoming a general officer.[132]

Likewise, AMC's efforts to place more air-mobility officers in staff positions are paying off. According to Brig Gen Robert R. Allardice, when he was a captain serving on the Air Staff in the mid-1980s, there were approximately five O-6 positions for airlifters.[133] When he returned to the Air Staff in the late 1990s, the situation had changed dramatically. Based on his observations, the number of air-mobility officers on the staff had increased, and they were serving in positions outside the traditional mobility track.[134] For example, as a colonel, General Allardice served on the Air Staff as chief of the War and Mobilization Plans Division and then helped develop and implement the EAF concept as chief of the Expeditionary Air Force Implementation Division. According to him, neither of those positions would have gone to a mobility officer in the 1980s.[135] His observation closely aligns with the actual number of colonels on the Air Staff today. Of its 130 rated officers, 43 percent are air-mobility officers. Similarly, air-mobility colonels fill 33 percent of the billets on the Joint Staff and 43 percent on the OSD staff. These statistics and observations further indicate that AMC's efforts to identify air-mobility officers at an early age and then track and place them in key broadening assignments constitute an effective program and a successful method of long-term deliberate leadership and force development.

This chapter discussed the rise of air-mobility generals in the post–Cold War era by first reviewing the unique mission expertise and competencies that air-mobility officers provide the nation. It then addressed the organizational and cultural changes in AMC that enabled the command to meet war fighters' needs efficiently and effectively. Finally, it examined how AMC deliberately develops leaders who not only fully understand air-mobility operations and the DTS but also have the right broadening opportunities so that they are more capable and sufficiently prepared to assume a greater role within the defense community and execute national security strategy. The next chapter advances the argument by discussing several factors that may affect the rise of air-mobility generals in the future.

Notes

1. Hutcheson, *Air Mobility*, 125.
2. Kross, "Air Mobility Symposium Address," 262.
3. Hutcheson, *Air Mobility*, 49. As evidence of the increase in deployments, "the U.S. Air Force participated in approximately 60 deployments in 1990 and *more than 650 in 1997*" (emphasis in original). Ibid.
4. Air Force Doctrine Document (AFDD) 2-6, *Air Mobility Operations*, i.
5. Johnson, transcript of interview, 89.
6. Quoted in AFDD 2-6, *Air Mobility Operations*, i.
7. Ibid.
8. Air Mobility Command, *2006 Air Mobility Master Plan*, 24.
9. Ibid., 23.
10. AFDD 2-6, *Air Mobility Operations*, 28.
11. Ibid., 29.
12. Ibid., 30.
13. Ibid.
14. Ibid.
15. Ibid., 31.
16. Ibid.
17. Ibid.
18. Ibid.
19. Ibid., 34.
20. Ibid.
21. Quoted in ibid. From October 2001 to January 2007, AMC airlifted 39,528 patients from Enduring Freedom and Iraqi Freedom. "The total number of evacuated patients since October 2001 is roughly equivalent to the population of Atlantic City, NJ." *U.S. Air Force AIM Points*.
22. AFDD 2-6, *Air Mobility Operations*, 35.
23. Ibid., 44.
24. Ibid.
25. Quoted in ibid., 45.
26. Self, interview.
27. AFDD 2-6, *Air Mobility Operations*, 46.
28. Ibid., 47.
29. Ibid., 47–48.
30. Ibid., 48.
31. Begert, "Kosovo and Theater Air Mobility," 12.
32. Ibid.
33. Ibid., 21.
34. AFDD 2-6, *Air Mobility Operations*, 56.
35. Ibid., 61.
36. Ibid.
37. Ibid.
38. Self, interview.
39. Shriver to the author, e-mail. The average daily sortie count from January 2003 to April 2006 was 220, 150 of which were mobility sorties.

40. Chow, *Peacetime Tempo of Air Mobility Operations*, xv.
41. Mets, "Between Two Worlds," 53.
42. Wynne, "Letter to Airmen."
43. Downing, "Mobility Air Forces," 47.
44. Self, interview.
45. Kross, interview.
46. Ibid.
47. Fogleman, interview.
48. Fogleman, transcript of interview, 8.
49. Ibid.
50. Hutcheson, *Air Mobility*, 52. "As the single manager for defense transportation in peace and war, it [USTRANSCOM] exercises combatant command over the Navy's Military Sealift Command (MSC), the Army's Military Traffic Management Command (MTMC) [renamed the Surface Deployment and Distribution Command (SDDC) in 2004], and the Air Force's Air Mobility Command." Ibid. As the DPO, USTRANSCOM is essentially the supply-chain manager for the DOD and has the authority to standardize technology as well as policies and thereby streamline the distribution process, which improves support to the combatant commanders.
51. Today, we have nine unified commands: United States Central Command, United States European Command, United States Southern Command, United States Pacific Command, United States Special Operations Command, United States Northern Command, United States Joint Forces Command, United States Strategic Command, and United States Transportation Command.
52. Handy, transcript of interview, 23.
53. Due to the increasing demands put on USTRANSCOM in the post–Cold War environment, the DOD decided in 2005 that the commander of USTRANSCOM and AMC would no longer be dual hatted. In July 2005, at the recommendation of General Handy, commander of USTRANSCOM and AMC, the secretary of defense split the commands; however, he continued to select two air-mobility generals—Gen Norton A. Schwartz and Gen Duncan J. McNabb—to lead USTRANSCOM and AMC, respectively.
54. Cassidy, transcript of interview, 70.
55. *Global Transportation Network*. "GTN gives its customers located anywhere in the world a seamless, near-real-time capability to access—and employ—transportation and deployment information. GTN is an automated command and control information system that supports the family of transportation users and providers, both [DOD] and commercial, by providing an integrated system of in-transit visibility information and command and control capabilities." Ibid.
56. History, Air Mobility Command (Provisional), vol. 1, 15 January–31 May 1992, 26.
57. Ibid.
58. Johnson, transcript of interview, 61.
59. Ibid., 86.
60. Quoted in Hutcheson, *Air Mobility*, 116.

61. Ibid., 38.
62. Hazdra, *Air Mobility*, 14.
63. Ibid., 81.
64. Sturkol, "Warfare Center."
65. Ibid.
66. Handy, transcript of interview, 168.
67. In 2006 the Mobility Weapons School realigned under the Air Force Warfare Center at Nellis AFB, Nevada.
68. Rosine, "Warfare Center Creates Mobility Warriors." Two of the seven former Air Mobility Warfare Center commanders earned a third star (Christopher Kelly and William Welser III), and one became a four-star general (William Begert).
69. Hutcheson, *Air Mobility*, 47.
70. Kross, transcript of interview, 16.
71. Wilkes, Stinnette, and Reed, "Expeditionary Mobility Task Force," 15.
72. Ibid., 16.
73. Ibid., 17.
74. Whittle, "Built for War."
75. Handy, transcript of interview, 9–10.
76. Ibid., 10–11. Although the Eighteenth Air Force commander was initially a three-star billet, it became a two-star in 2005 because after USTRANSCOM and AMC split, the latter had to come up with a four-star billet. Consequently, it chose to give up its three-star position at Eighteenth Air Force to create a four-star position at AMC. According to General Handy, both the Air Force chief of staff and the secretary of the Air Force said they would reestablish the Eighteenth Air Force position as a three-star billet at the next opportunity. Ibid., 3.
77. Fogleman, transcript of interview, 3.
78. Self, interview. Brigadier General Self was the assistant executive officer to General Fogleman from 1992 to 1993. When he heard that General Fogleman was going to be the new AMC commander, he said to himself, "Oh no, not a fighter pilot." However, he soon realized that General Fogleman was a visionary general officer who was ultimately responsible for creating the mobility culture prevalent in AMC today.
79. Fogleman, transcript of interview, 3.
80. Ibid.
81. Fogleman, interview.
82. Fogleman, transcript of interview, 3.
83. Ibid., 42.
84. Fogleman, interview.
85. Kelly, interview.
86. Fogleman, transcript of interview, 42.
87. Fogleman, interview.
88. Cassidy, transcript of interview, 145.
89. Fogleman, interview.
90. Ibid.

91. Ibid. The plastic spoon that General Fogleman referred to was from the box lunches that airlifters bought in the flight kitchen before long, overseas missions. A spoon in the pocket was more commonly associated with strategic versus tactical airlifters and is today generally considered an outdated, negative image of the mobility community.
92. Kross, interview.
93. Fogleman, transcript of interview, 44.
94. Mets, "Between Two Worlds," 42.
95. Ibid., 46.
96. Ibid., 47.
97. Ibid., 43.
98. Kross, transcript of interview, 23.
99. Ibid.
100. Mets, "Between Two Worlds," 48.
101. Ibid., 47.
102. Larsen, "Air Mobility Culture."
103. Handy, transcript of interview, 165.
104. Handy, interview.
105. Volant Spotlight was the MAJCOM version of the Air Force–level Air Staff Training (ASTRA) Program, a highly selective internship designed to give captains from many different career fields exposure to the Air Staff and other senior staffs within the DOD. Today, 17 of 51 air-mobility generals are ASTRA graduates.
106. Fogleman, transcript of interview, 5.
107. Ibid.
108. Ibid.
109. Brown, "Sources of Leadership Doctrine," 44.
110. Weaver, *Developing Aerospace Leaders*, 52.
111. Fitzhugh, interview.
112. Concerned about the development of future leaders, Gen Michael E. Ryan, Air Force chief of staff, stood up the Developing Aerospace Leaders (DAL) office in March 2000. The purpose of the DAL initiative was to

> [establish] processes and procedures that build a senior leadership corps able to
> - understand national security interests and fully exploit the aerospace domain to support national objectives;
> - develop, cultivate, and maintain operational competence in the medium of aerospace;
> - envision, develop, acquire, sustain, support, and employ capabilities that exploit the aerospace domain to create military effects; and
> - communicate the absolute and relative value of aerospace capabilities to the American people and their representatives.

Thirtle, "Developing Aerospace Leaders," 53–54. Today, deliberate leadership and force development are being institutionalized throughout the Air Force, which published its first leadership-development doctrine, AFDD 1-1, *Leadership and Force Development*, in 2004. The Air Force also recently instituted the development team (DT) concept. Each career field has a DT that provides short- and long-term assignment vectors based on inputs from commanders, desires of the service members, and needs of the Air Force. The goal is to deliberately develop individuals so that they are sufficiently broadened throughout their careers.

113. According to many senior officers interviewed by the author, there are several possible reasons why other commands, such as ACC, did not initiate officer-development programs similar to AMC's. One of the more provocative reasons was that because fighter pilots already ran the Air Force, ACC did not need to develop its officers aggressively. Another reason was that developmental programs cost money and that ACC would rather spend its money in other areas. One of the more common reasons was that fighter and bomber aircraft are more difficult to fly and require more years to master; therefore, young fighter and bomber pilots cannot afford broadening assignments outside the cockpit until they are more senior in grade. This reasoning, however, does not explain the willingness of ACC to send its best young officers to the two-year Air Force Intern Program (AFIP), a highly selective, nonflying internship designed to give young officers with four to six years of service experience on the Air Staff, Joint Staff, or Office of the Secretary of Defense staff.

114. Fogleman, transcript of interview, 5.
115. Fogleman, interview.
116. Ibid.
117. Begert, interview.
118. Kross, "Air Mobility Symposium Address," 259.
119. Begert, interview.
120. Ibid.
121. Ibid.
122. Ibid.
123. Seiler, "Point Paper on Phoenix Horizon."
124. Ibid. AMC is the only MAJCOM that travels to the intermediate and senior developmental schools as well as the combatant-commander staffs in order to personally meet with air-mobility officers and hiring officials to discuss future assignments. Col Richard E. Fitzhugh Jr., AMC's former deputy director of personnel, said this was an effective way not only to introduce air-mobility personnel to the value of volunteering for broadening assignments outside the traditional mobility-type jobs but also to establish relationships with the combatant commands and better explain to hiring officials the experiences and competencies that air-mobility officers bring to their staffs. Fitzhugh, interview.

125. Due to budgetary constraints, the Air Force decided in 2006 to change the focus of the AFIP and restructure it to make it part of intermediate developmental education (IDE). The change in the AFIP had the secondary effect of changing AMC's Phoenix Hawk program, AMC's version of the AFIP. For reasons unclear to the author, AMC had to disband its own intern program following the change in the AFIP's focus. AMC, however, fought to maintain part of the developmental program that it had managed for the past 13 years. Consequently, five of the 35 officers selected for the new IDE-equivalent AFIP are designated to come to AMC, which is currently the only MAJCOM to have AFIP interns on the staff. The new AMC program is a one-year internship

followed by a staff tour of 24–36 months on the USTRANSCOM or AMC staff. Kenner, "Talking Paper on Air Force Intern Program (AMC)."

126. Seiler, "Point Paper on Phoenix Hawk."
127. Seiler, "Point Paper on Phoenix Mobility."
128. Seiler, "Point Paper on Phoenix Reach."
129. Burgess, interview.
130. Whitehouse to author, e-mail. According to Major Whitehouse, although ACC is adopting a centralized squadron-commander-selection-board process in 2007, the centralized board's philosophy will not differ significantly from that of the ACC board. Therefore, in terms of leadership development, it is worth mentioning the differences between the ACC and AMC squadron-commander-board philosophies. In general, ACC follows a decentralized-control/decentralized-execution model, whereas the AMC model resembles centralized control and centralized execution. ACC's philosophy is that the wing commander has primary hiring authority and often knows whom he wants to hire before the board meets. Therefore, the board process serves as a quality check of the wing leadership's game plan as well as an opportunity for wings to identify potential quality candidates for leadership positions. After publishing the squadron-commander list, ACC has virtually no say in who gets hired or by whom. There are two potential problems with this approach. First, in some ways it affirms the "old-boy network" / "it's not what you know, it's who knows you" perception. According to Major Whitehouse, wing commanders' assessments of leadership potential receive more emphasis than the nominees' records because "to a much higher degree than is the case in the mobility world, CAF squadron commanders must function as—and be perceived as—someone who literally leads the unit into combat." In fact, the bottom-line question ACC charges the squadron-commander board members to ask themselves is, "Could I sleep at night knowing that this officer is commanding one of my squadrons?" The second problem with this approach is that decentralizing the hiring process essentially removes any long-term game plans for ACC personnel. This makes it harder to deliberately develop and broaden ACC officers over time. Compared to ACC's squadron-selection-board process, AMC's is extremely centralized, whereby board members select candidates based more on their records and less on their preferences of whom they want to hire. Once the list is finalized, AMC commanders can bid for candidates on the list, but the AMC Eighteenth Air Force commander ultimately determines who goes where. This approach has the advantage of allowing AMC to identify, track, and place mobility people based on a long-term game plan. The problem with this approach is that it is very time consuming and labor intensive to track and place individuals in the command billets and their follow-on assignments. In addition, the process takes away a great deal of the hiring authority from the wing leadership. Although both the ACC and AMC processes have their faults, the author believes that AMC's process is more in line with the Air Force's deliberate force-development philosophy and has greater long-term benefits. A more structured, deliberate leadership-development program helps reduce prejudices and ensures that AMC and the Air Force are better postured for the future.

131. Burgess, interview.
132. CY 1998–CY 2006 AMC colonel promotion results briefing slides.
133. Allardice, interview.
134. Ibid.
135. Ibid.

Chapter 4

The Future of Mobility Generals

In the post–Cold War, postnuclear world, the real strategic military headquarters is not the Strategic Air Command at Offutt AFB in Nebraska, but the United States Transportation Command at Scott AFB, Illinois.

—Col Harry Summers, USA

The previous chapters described the interaction between changes in the geopolitical environment and the air-mobility community, which fostered an increase of mobility operations and a rise of mobility generals in the post–Cold War era. As the world and the air-mobility community continue to change, the question remains whether the number of air-mobility generals and their contributions will gain momentum and continue to rise in the years to come. Since it is hard to predict the future, this chapter considers two alternative horizons. First, it outlines why air-mobility generals will continue to advance and assume senior roles within the defense community. Second, it examines why the rise of air-mobility generals may be limited, implying that they have risen as high as they can within the Air Force and the national security establishment.

Air-Mobility Generals Will Continue to Rise

The complexities of the new world order already are placing a premium on airlift, which long has lived in the shadows of its more glamorous bomber and fighter forces. But since February 1991, there has been little air-to-air combat and few bombs dropped in anger. Even with the movement of so many fighters and bombers to Iraq, the role of airlift has moved into the spotlight and likely will stay there.

—Prof. Dennis Drew

THE FUTURE OF MOBILITY GENERALS

> *I believe we will be in the Middle East for a very long time yet.*
>
> —Gen T. Michael Moseley, USAF Chief of Staff

The most compelling reason why air-mobility generals will continue to succeed is that the air-mobility mission and the demand for air-mobility expertise will persist.[1] No other country has or will have in the near future an air-mobility capability like that of the United States. There is every reason to believe that "military forces, inter-agencies, non-governmental organizations, international organizations, and military allies" will continue to place a high demand on air-mobility capabilities in future geopolitical environments.[2] According to General Kross, AMC's capabilities and its leaders will continue to be in high demand—in fact, will continue to be the first in and the last out across the full spectrum of operations—because "human nature will never change. And the laws of physics will never change."[3] In other words, the world will always be a dangerous place, and as long as the United States continues to engage throughout the world, it must maintain a robust air-mobility capability. It follows that it should also grow and promote air-mobility generals who can lead complex air-mobility operations in an environment characterized by rapidly developing conflicts, humanitarian emergencies, and natural disasters.

The continued need for leaders with air-mobility expertise is particularly evident, considering future operations in Iraq. Despite recent public and congressional demands for troop withdrawals, there is little indication that the United States will pull out of the conflict anytime soon. On the contrary, in January 2007 Pres. George W. Bush announced a revised strategy for Iraq that included plans to add more than 20,000 troops for a "new approach to clearing, holding, and rebuilding Baghdad, neighborhood by neighborhood."[4] The addition of more ground troops will place increased demands on air mobility in the near future. Referring to the impact of the troop surge on air-mobility operations, a C-130 flight engineer remarked, "How are they going to get them there? Airlift. How are they going to feed them? Airlift. How are they going to bring them bullets? Airlift."[5] In other words, intertheater deployment, redeployment, and resupply airlift efforts; intratheater airlift of troops and supplies around the battlefield; and aeromedical evacuation of casualties will likely increase as a result of the troop surge. There will also be a greater demand for air-refueling capabilities because of the expected increase in close-air-support missions. Likewise, when the troop surge ends—and even further in the future, when most US ground troops redeploy—the demand for air-mobility operations will remain high due to the likelihood that the United States will provide air-mobility support for Iraqi ground troops as they take on a greater role in the counterinsurgency operation.

Current and future operations in Iraq point to the broader matter of air mobility's role in the GWOT in a future environment characterized by counterinsurgency operations and other forms of small and irregular wars. These are the most likely conflicts that the United States will face in the near- to midterm future. Although it is dangerous to assume that the next war will be exactly like the last, many military experts argue that the majority of conflicts in "the next fifty years will be irregular warfare in an 'Arc of Instability' that encompasses much of the greater Middle East and part of Africa and Central and South Asia."[6] Likewise, a RAND study of 2006 finds that "it is relatively easy to declare that insurgent threats have grown in importance relative to conventional ones in recent years and that this situation is not likely to change in the near future, for the simple reason that the number of serious conventional military threats to U.S. interests has declined substantially."[7]

In these types of conflicts, the support roles of airpower, such as transport and reconnaissance, are "usually the most important and effective [airpower] missions."[8] In fact, "tactical battlefield mobility, including casualty evacuation . . . and logistics support for surface combat units, is a vital airpower function for maintaining security and neutralizing hostile forces during [counterinsurgency] and combating terrorism operations."[9] This is true because the center of gravity in small wars is often the civil population, and ground troops—as opposed to airpower—play a greater role in winning the hearts and minds of the people. Airpower's main contribution, therefore, is to support the ground troops. "In numerous counterinsurgency campaigns, the ability to airlift army and police units to remote locations and to keep them supplied by airdrop and helicopter has proven decisive."[10] Likewise, unlike conventional conflicts, which rely on the destructive capabilities of combat aircraft, small wars benefit more from the constructive effects of airpower. According to the Marine Corps' *Small Wars Manual*, the "motive in small wars is not material destruction. It is usually a project dealing with the social, economic, and political development of the people."[11] Air mobility, therefore, is ideally suited for this type of support mission. For example, air mobility can help nation-building efforts by airlifting supplies and support personnel such as civil engineers to rebuild roads, schools, and basic infrastructure.[12] It can also assist the local population by transporting "ballots and election monitors" and by air-dropping humanitarian supplies.[13]

Air mobility also plays a key role in rebuilding a nation's air force through foreign internal defense (FID) operations. In fact, an air-mobility pilot—General Allardice—is the current commander of the Coalition Air Force Transition Team, which is responsible for standing up the Iraqi air force. Mobility officers are well prepared for these types of positions for several reasons, including (a) their experience in flying in the theater of operations, (b) their expertise in dealing with senior foreign-military officers, and (c) the fact that most of the countries vulnerable to insurgencies and small wars cannot afford (nor does the United States want them to acquire) high-tech combat aircraft. Rather, a developing nation's air force usually consists of less-expensive support aircraft such as the C-130, reconnaissance platforms, and helicopters. Air-mobility experts, therefore, are well suited to train and stand up a developing nation's air force.

In addition to providing FID and counterinsurgency support in irregular-warfare operations, air mobility will also continue to play a key role in other future missions. Due to the laws of nature and as long as the United States is willing to engage with the rest of the world, a need will always exist for air mobility to provide support during domestic and international humanitarian emergencies such as Hurricane Katrina and tsunami-relief operations. Future international-relief missions have the added benefit of boosting the US image abroad. For instance, following the deployment of an AMC contingency response group in the aftermath of the Pakistani earthquake in 2005, the US approval rating in Pakistan increased from 23 to 46 percent, according to a poll conducted by the Washington-based nonprofit organization Terror Free Tomorrow.[14] This increase in US approval rating is important because it can have a long-term positive impact on US-Pakistani relations and an even greater effect on US strategy for combating the GWOT.

Similarly, due to the Pentagon's proposal to continue reducing personnel strength at overseas bases, air-mobility resources and expertise will remain in high demand during future crisis situations that require rapid troop deployment or show-of-force missions.[15] The DOD's emphasis on replacing the overseas Cold War base structure with a network of expeditionary bases will require senior leaders to further draw on air-mobility experts trained in opening and conducting bare-base operations. In addition, if the United States continues to "go it alone," as it has in recent operations, it may not be able to depend on overflight or landing rights in the future, which will increase air-refueling operations and create a need for tanking expertise to plan most overseas deployments.[16]

Air mobility will also likely play an important role in the success of United States Africa Command, which stood up in early 2007. Due to the strategic importance of Africa in combating the GWOT, the Bush administration created this command to oversee security cooperation, build partnership capability, provide defense support to nonmilitary missions, and conduct military operations on the African continent.[17] Similar to missions in Iraq, future air operations in Africa will focus less on destruction and more on construction efforts in order to avoid the long-term consequences of weak and failing states. "To check the communist and Islamic expansionism," according to H. John Poole, a counterinsurgency expert and former US marine, "the West will need nothing short of a modern Marshall Plan."[18] Air-mobility experts, therefore, will be vital to the success of opening expeditionary bases and conducting humanitarian and peacekeeping operations involving the rapid transport of supplies, troops, and international-aid organizations directly to villages and communities. Direct delivery will be a key element in the success of these operations due to the corrupt nature of many African countries. Likewise, some defense experts believe that Africa "could be a major growth area for C-130 traffic because of the need to move more people and materiel into the region."[19] Therefore, air-mobility experts could also play an important role in future FID operations in Africa.

Besides future missions in Africa, air mobility will continue to play a key role and remain the primary interface of the Air Force with the joint community.[20] According to General Fogleman, when General Handy was the commander of AMC, his reputation with the Army was the best of any Air Force officer—partly because of the relationships he established and maintained throughout his career with soldiers that he transported and air-dropped out of the back of his C-130. Consequently, when General Handy's name appeared on the short list to assume command of AMC and USTRANSCOM, the Army chief of staff gave him "two thumbs up."[21] Gen Duncan McNabb, the AMC commander, and Gen Norton Schwartz, the USTRANSCOM commander, have similar reputations, according to General Fogleman—which is important because the greater the involvement of air-mobility generals with the rest of the defense establishment, the greater their chance of being considered for unified-command positions within the joint community.[22]

The number of air-mobility generals may also rise because of the increased use of robotic aircraft, also known as unmanned aerial vehicles (UAV). The use of these aircraft increased dramatically during operations in Iraq and Afghanistan. "UAV flying hours have increased from less than 20,000 in 2001 to more than 160,000 in 2006."[23] Although smaller UAVs flew most of the hours, the current trend and technological developments indicate that they will continue to fly more strike and reconnaissance missions, thereby further reducing the need for many types of manned combat and combat-support aircraft. This could lead to a major reshaping of the Air Force's aircraft inventory and may be one of the reasons that "the Defense Department may have been cutting back on manned aircraft programs—particularly fighters such as the USAF's F/A-22 and the joint service F-35—because defense leaders believe that equally powerful but cheaper unmanned replacements could be around the corner."[24]

A decrease in manned combat and reconnaissance aircraft requirements could lead to consolidation of ACC's command structure and fewer command opportunities for officers in the CAF. The question of whether senior CAF leaders have the same regard for commanding a UAV unit as they do for commanding a manned-aircraft squadron remains unanswered at this time. However, in the event that they do not, in light of fewer command opportunities with regard to manned aircraft, officers in the CAF may find themselves less competitive for general-officer billets than officers in the air-mobility community—the last community that will transition to UAVs.[25] Consequently, the number of air-mobility generals relative to CAF generals within the defense community may increase in the future.

Precision-guided munitions (PGM), another technological advance, may facilitate the rise of mobility generals. Today, the CAF is the primary means of delivering PGMs. However, no technological reasons prevent mobility aircraft from assuming a greater role in bringing about the same kinetic effects as strike aircraft using PGMs. For instance, a C-130 is currently capable of delivering the GBU-43/B—the largest-ever satellite-guided, air-delivered weapon.[26] As more mobility aircraft become capable of delivering PGMs, the Air Force will have less need to purchase and maintain expensive strike aircraft. Consequently, because the number of senior leaders in the CAF will decrease, the Air Force will need to promote mobility generals.

Finally, the future of air-mobility generals is bright because of AMC's continued focus on the professional development of its leaders. According to General Allardice, AMC excels at identifying potential leaders, tracking them in a database, and providing them with the right broadening experiences in order to prepare them to become effective general officers.[27] AMC is just now beginning to see the results of deliberate force development as the first beneficiaries of that program begin to reach senior-officer rank. However, based on the proven success of its legacy Phoenix Horizon programs and on its rigorous process of selecting and placing squadron commanders, AMC is poised to continue developing a large resource pool of air-mobility leaders. Perhaps more important than an increase in the actual numbers of air-mobility generals, however, AMC's emphasis on leadership development will have an even broader, more far-reaching effect. As General Fogleman remarked, each year, air-mobility officers continue to "up their game" and outperform their predecessors. This healthy competition will continue to benefit the air-mobility community and the defense establishment well into the future.[28]

Air-Mobility Generals Will Not Continue to Rise

The service's purpose is to generate combat capability that protects the country, and not necessarily to provide equal career opportunities for those who fly heavies, or, heaven forbid, don't wear wings at all.

—Gen Merrill McPeak

The only thing harder than getting a new idea into the military mind is to get the old one out.

—Sir Basil H. Liddell Hart

Although the air-mobility mission and demand for expertise will persist, this does not necessarily mean that air-mobility generals will assume more senior-leadership positions within the defense community. For instance, although senior leaders recognized the strategically important role that air mobility and its leaders played during the Berlin airlift, the Air Force did not subsequently promote more airlift pilots to senior-leadership positions. In fact, another 50 years passed before the Air Force assigned another air-mobility officer above the rank of major general to the European theater of operations. Air Force culture may explain this lag. Broadly speaking, *culture* is "the set of shared attitudes, values, goals, and practices that characterizes an institution or organization" a definition gleaned from a standard dictionary. Like many organizations, the Air Force selects its leaders from an elite cadre of individuals closely associated with the organization's core mission, which, for most of the Air Force's history, involved flying combat airplanes. Therefore, for the past 60 years, the overwhelming majority of officers considered contenders for senior-leadership positions have been combat pilots. Specifically, every Air Force chief of staff since 1947 has been either a bomber or (more recently) a fighter pilot. In his book *Rise of the Fighter Generals: The Problem of Air Force Leadership, 1945–1982*, Mike Worden described the transformation of senior Air Force leadership from the bomber to the fighter community. In that study, he argued that fighter pilots rose to preeminence over bomber pilots because the bomber generals failed to adjust to the realities of a growing conventional Soviet threat and the failures of the war in Vietnam.[29] Consequently, beginning in the early 1960s, bomber generals began to lose their hold on top leadership positions and officially turned over the reins to the fighter community in 1982 when a fighter pilot, Gen Charles A. Gabriel, became Air Force chief of staff. More than 25 years after assuming command, fighter pilots continue to lead the Air Force.

Worden's study illustrates two key points. First, throughout the Air Force's entire history, only pilots who flew combat aircraft have led that service. This fact has undoubtedly created an organizational norm and a cultural mind-set that assumes this is the way it should always be.[30] Second, it took 20 years and a significant emotional event like the failure in Vietnam for the Air Force to effect a modicum of cultural change and alter the composition of its senior leadership. Hence, the future rise of air-mobility generals may proceed very slowly or perhaps not at all, absent a significant military failure like Vietnam. Unless senior leaders perceive operations in Iraq and Afghanistan as failures of the same magnitude as Vietnam, Air Force senior leaders may well maintain the status quo. Edgar Schein's analysis of organizational change supports this conclusion: "If an organization has had a long history of success with certain assumptions about itself and the environment, it is unlikely to want to challenge or reexamine those assumptions."[31] Likewise, in his discussion of successful innovations in military organizations, Stephen Rosen contends that unless senior leaders perceive the need for change, it will not occur.[32]

Other factors favor the status quo of senior Air Force leaders. According to Schein, senior leaders have "a great deal of power to influence the choice of their successor," and there is a tendency in organizations for leadership to "blindly perpetuate" itself.[33] General Handy confirmed that when it comes to selecting people for senior-leadership positions, "there is a strong temptation to clone yourself and select people with the same background and experiences. It is human nature to do this; however, it does not benefit the organization to constantly surround yourself with people that think like you do."[34] General Fogleman also remarked that his mentor told him that as chief, Fogleman's primary purpose in life was to groom his successor. But he felt it was his duty to develop leaders who did not look exactly like him and thus give the institution a variety of options.[35] Unless other senior leaders adopt a similar attitude toward senior-leadership development and selection, air-mobility generals may not rise any higher in the future.

Yet another obstacle to air-mobility generals may be the laws governing general-officer billets and promotions. According to Title X, chapter 32, the Air Force is limited to 279 general-officer billets or "headspace." Of those 279 generals, no more than 15.7 percent may have more than two stars and no more than 25 percent of that number may have four stars. This equates to 43 three-star and 10 four-star Air Force generals.[36] The Air Force may have more than 10 four-star generals if it has officers serving in a joint four-star position. Similarly, it may have fewer than 43 three-stars at any given time in order to promote an additional brigadier or major general. To increase headspace, the Air Force must petition Congress to change the law—an extremely rare occurrence. Therefore, in order for the Air Force to promote more air-mobility generals, it would have to promote fewer generals from other communities, something not always possible because of the Air Force's organizational structure. For example, ACC has four numbered air forces compared to only one in AMC. Each numbered air force is led by a three-star general and a one-star vice-commander. Based on this fact alone, ACC's numbered air forces garner eight general-officer billets compared to AMC's two. This not only limits AMC's ability to develop one- and two-star generals to become three- and four-star generals but also limits the command's ability to stratify its senior officers.

In addition, according to Brig Gen (sel) Cathy Clothier, director of Air Force General Officer Management, the Air Force is currently positioning itself to develop more general officers and create more billets for them in the cyberspace and intelligence career fields.[37] Furthermore, Lt Gen David Deptula, the new Air Force deputy chief of staff for intelligence, surveillance, and reconnaissance, has said that he is working to "expand the number of Air Force general-officer intelligence billets, help position Air Force personnel to fill important joint and national level intelligence billets, and organize intelligence as an 'Air Force–wide enterprise.'"[38] To expand the number of billets in these emerging mission areas, the Air Force must take some away from other career fields. In other words, the Air Force cannot increase the size of the pie, a fact which, combined with other organizational limitations, may affect the future increase of air-mobility generals.

For another constraining factor, one may look to the limited number of designated air-mobility billets on the Joint Staff. Goldwater-Nichols requires that all officers complete a joint-duty tour before becoming generals. Thus, air-mobility officers may find themselves at a disadvantage due to the limited number of joint positions allocated to them. For example, of 12 rated officers currently serving on the Joint Staff in the Pentagon, only two have an air-mobility background. Fighter and bomber officers fill nine of the positions, and a special-operations officer occupies the remaining slot. According to General Allardice, the joint community often designates a position for a fighter or a bomber pilot when in fact any rated officer can fill the position.[39] Air-mobility generals will be at a disadvantage as long as the joint community continues to maintain this attitude. Besides the number of joint billets, fewer command opportunities and billets for air-mobility officers exist in the Middle East, compared to officers in the CAF. Of the 14 permanent-party, senior-officer positions, air-mobility officers fill four of them; a bomber pilot and a contracting officer each fill a billet; and fighter pilots fill the remaining eight positions.

This situation may result in fewer opportunities for air-mobility leaders to establish credibility with their counterparts in the CAF and other services. This is important because leaders often hire and promote people they know. Moreover, limited assignment opportunities in the Middle East constrain air-mobility officers' exposure to combat-fighter operations. If air-mobility generals wish to continue their rise, according to General Fogleman, they should gain a better understanding of the fighter world.[40] General Begert confirms that his prior knowledge of CAF operations helped ease his transition from air-mobility officer to commander of PACAF.[41]

Lastly, air-mobility generals may face limited prospects because of self-imposed restraints. Several years have gone by since General Begert served as PACAF commander, and with each passing year, his groundbreaking achievement fades further into the background. Not until another air-mobility general breaks the glass ceiling will some air-mobility officers think they have a chance to lead combat organizations or reach the most senior levels of leadership within the defense community. By setting self-imposed limits on what they can achieve, air-mobility officers themselves may represent the main obstacle to their own advancement.

Notes

1. Kross, "Air Mobility Symposium Address," 262.
2. Hutcheson, *Air Mobility*, 126.
3. Kross, "Air Mobility Symposium Address," 262.
4. Lubold, "Forward Surge!"
5. Quoted in Bryant, "Airlift's Wild Ride."
6. Nagl, *Learning to Eat Soup with a Knife*, xvi.
7. Vick et al., *Air Power in the New Counterinsurgency Era*, 57.
8. Corum and Johnson, *Airpower in Small Wars*, 427.
9. Air Force Doctrine Document (AFDD) 2-3.1, *Foreign Internal Defense*, 24.
10. Corum and Johnson, *Airpower in Small Wars*, 427.
11. Quoted in Bellflower, "Indirect Approach," 37.
12. Ibid., 38.
13. Ibid.
14. Whittle, "Built for War."
15. Isenberg, "U.S. Global Posture Review." In 2004, as part of its transformation efforts, the Bush administration announced the results of its Global Posture Review, which proposed withdrawing as many as 70,000 troops stationed in Europe and Asia as part of a major troop realignment. The purpose of the realignment was to reconfigure the military's global footprint to reflect changes in the geopolitical environment. In the future, the Defense Department will rely less on traditional large, fixed bases overseas and more on smaller "lily pads" in places such as Uzbekistan, Pakistan, Qatar, and Djibouti.
16. Narvid, *Tanker-Force Structure*, 22.
17. Garamone, "DoD Establishing U.S. Africa Command."
18. Quoted in Fabey, "African Command Good First Step."
19. Ibid.
20. Fogleman, interview.
21. Ibid.
22. Ibid.
23. Hockmuth, "UAVs—the Next Generation," 73.
24. Tirpak, "Will We Have an Unmanned Armada?" 4.
25. Ibid.
26. "GBU-43/B 'Mother of All Bombs.'"

27. Allardice, interview.
28. Fogleman, interview.
29. Norden, "Changing of the Guard," 60–66.
30. The author's experience and several interviews for this paper reveal that this is a fairly common belief among many Air Force members.
31. Schein, *Organizational Culture and Leadership*, 321.
32. Rosen, *Winning the Next War*, 96.
33. Schein, *Organizational Culture and Leadership*, 378–79.
34. Handy, interview.
35. Fogleman, interview.
36. The Air Force currently has 13 four-star generals, four of whom are serving in joint billets in United States Transportation Command, United States Joint Forces Command, United States Northern Command, and as director of the CIA. The joint billets do not count against the total allowable Air Force four-star billets.
37. Clothier, interview.
38. Quoted in Putrich, "USAF Reorganizing Intelligence Command," 15.
39. Allardice, interview.
40. Fogleman, interview.
41. Begert, interview.

Chapter 5

Conclusions

It has been convincingly demonstrated that strategic airlift can be mobilized quickly and employed at far-distant points as a powerful and effective component of American airpower. Our strategic airlift component has attained our national objectives in peacetime. The airlift component has now taken the proper place alongside the combat strategic, tactical and air defense components of airpower. Unlike those armed components, the airlift component can be employed independently in time of peace or in time of war.

—Gen Laurence S. Kuter, 1949

Air-mobility generals may or may not continue to flourish. The most compelling reason why they will maintain their rise is the fact that the world is a dangerous place and that the nation's national security strategy will likely persist in putting a premium on air mobility and air-mobility expertise. Based on the important role that air-mobility experts will play in the GWOT, FID, irregular warfare, and humanitarian operations, and as long as AMC continues to broadly develop a pool of officers with high potential, the Air Force will likely extend its practice of promoting and placing air-mobility generals in positions of increasing authority.[1]

On the other hand, air-mobility generals may have risen as far as they possibly can, perhaps due to the natural tendency for organizations to maintain the status quo and resist cultural and organizational change. It is also possible that the rise of air-mobility generals will slow in the future as the Air Force builds up its general-officer corps in other mission areas, such as intelligence and cyberspace. The Air Force may work around this problem by petitioning Congress to change the laws and increase the number of general-officer positions; however, the likelihood of successfully garnering more senior-officer billets is slim, considering that the Air Force is drawing down in order to recapitalize the force.

Increasing the number of general-officer billets will not serve the long-term interests of the Air Force if doing so only encourages the status quo. In fact, it may be time to make bold decisions regarding what kind of officer will provide the most effective leadership for the United States Air Force and the nation. This paper showed why and how air-mobility generals are poised to lead the Air Force in the twenty-first century, mostly by positing air mobility as the great enabler for other Air Force, Defense Department, and national missions. But this has been merely the argument's animation. Just as Mahan and Mitchell used the language of battleships and bombers to enliven their ideas of maritime and air and space power, this paper has enlisted the language of support and logistics to rouse from the minds of men and women the true purpose of airpower. To borrow a famous phrase, this paper holds as its logic the use of the air and maintains as its grammar the control of the medium.[2] The purpose of airpower is not to shoot other planes from the sky; it is to use the air in a manner consistent with national interests. Eighty years ago, Mitchell's broad concept of airpower provided a theoretical basis for the emergence of the United States as an air and space nation. Today, in the post–Cold War era, the air *is* the great commons. Within the United States Air Force, the air-mobility community best leverages this reality. Changes in the geopolitical environment and the increased frequency of mobility-centric operations indicate that mobility no longer plays a secondary role in airpower strategy. As the Air Force's core mission shifts, both a strong contingent of senior leaders with air-mobility expertise and a global worldview should remain in place. AMC's focus on adapting its organization and developing a robust cadre of leaders who have the right mix of competencies and experiences indicates that mobility leaders are prepared to continue rising to meet the challenges within the Air Force, throughout the nation, and across the globe.

Notes

1. The most recent brigadier-general selection board supports this conclusion—24 percent of the 29 officers selected for promotion were mobility officers
2. Clausewitz, *On War*, 605.

Bibliography

Primary Sources

Allardice, Brig Gen Robert R., director, Airman Development and Sustainment, Deputy Chief of Staff, Manpower and Personnel, Washington, DC. Interview by the author, 22 February 2007.

Bash, Brig Gen Brooks, director of combat and information operations, Global Operations Directorate, United States Strategic Command, Offutt AFB, NE. Interview by the author, 30 March 2007.

Begert, Gen William J., former commander, Pacific Air Forces, and air component commander for the commander in chief, United States Pacific Command, Hickam AFB, HI. Interview by the author, 12 February 2007.

Bell, Capt Aaron, AF/DPG, Washington, DC. To the author. E-mail, 23 January–1 May 2007.

———. Interview by the author, 6 February 2007.

Brady, Lt Gen Roger, deputy chief of staff, manpower and personnel, Headquarters US Air Force, Washington, DC. Interview by the author, 21 January 2007.

Burgess, Capt Cornell, Headquarters AMC/A1FD, Scott AFB, IL. Interview by the author, 27 March 2007.

Clothier, Brig Gen (sel) Cathy, director, Air Force General Officer Management, Deputy Chief of Staff, Manpower and Personnel, Washington, DC. Interview by the author, 2 February 2007.

Fitzhugh, Col Richard E., Jr., former deputy director of personnel, Air Mobility Command, Scott AFB, IL. Interview by the author, 10 February 2007.

Fogleman, Gen Ronald R., former chief of staff, United States Air Force, Washington, DC. Interview by the author, 2 February 2007.

Fullhart, Brig Gen Randal, deputy chief, Central Security Service, National Security Agency, Fort George G. Meade, MD. Interview by the author, 8 April 2007.

Handy, Gen John W., former commander in chief, United States Transportation Command, and commander, Air Mobility

Command, Scott AFB, IL. Interview by the author, 29 January 2007.

Hartford, Lt Col Darren, Headquarters AMC/A1L, Scott AFB, IL. Interview by the author, 31 January 2007.

Hoagland, Lt Col Bradley, Headquarters AMC/A1FD, Scott AFB, IL. Interview by the author, 31 January 2007.

Kelly, Lt Gen Christopher A., vice-commander, Air Mobility Command, Scott AFB, IL. Interview by the author, 31 January 2007.

Kross, Gen Walter, former commander in chief, United States Transportation Command, and commander, Air Mobility Command, Scott AFB, IL. Interview by the author, 30 January 2007.

Lorenz, Lt Gen Stephen, commander, Air University, Maxwell AFB, AL. Interview by the author, 19 January 2007.

Mast, Mr. Paul, Headquarters AMC/A1FD, Scott AFB, IL. Interview by the author, 31 January 2007.

McNabb, Gen Duncan, commander, Air Mobility Command, Scott AFB, IL. Interview by the author, 22 May 2007.

Moorehead, Gen Glen "Wally," III, former commander, North Atlantic Treaty Organization, Allied Air Component Command, Izmir, Turkey, and commander, Sixteenth Air Force, United States Air Forces in Europe, Ramstein AB, Germany. Interview by the author, 8 March 2007.

Nolte, Lt Col William, Headquarters ACC/A1FD, Langley AFB, VA. Interview by the author, 15 March 2007.

Self, Brig Gen Kip, commander, 314th Airlift Wing, Little Rock AFB, AR. Interview by the author, 20 March 2007.

Service, Mr. John, AF/DPG, Washington, DC. To the author. E-mail, 16 April 2007.

Shriver, Maj Todd, Air Mobility Division analyst, combined air operations center, Al Udeid AB, Doha, Qatar. To the author. E-mail, 30 January 2007.

Whitehouse, Maj Evan, Headquarters ACC/A1FD, Langley AFB, VA. To the author. E-mail, 15 March 2007.

Wuesthoff, Brig Gen Scott, vice-commander, tanker airlift control center, Scott AFB, IL. Interview by the author, 31 January 2007.

Secondary Sources

"Air Cargo Statistics, U.S. Commercial Air Carriers: Fiscal Years 1970–2003." Washington, DC: Federal Aviation Administration, Office of Aviation Policy and Plans, 2003. http://www.aia-aerospace.org/stats/facts_figures/ff_04_05/FF04P083.pdf.

Air Force Doctrine Document 1-1. "Leadership and Force Development." Draft revision, 2007.

Air Force Doctrine Document 2-3.1. *Foreign Internal Defense*, 15 September 2007.

Air Force Doctrine Document 2-6. *Air Mobility Operations*, 1 March 2006.

Air Mobility Command. *2006 Air Mobility Master Plan*. Scott AFB, IL: AMC, April 2006.

Aspin, Les. *Report on the Bottom-Up Review*, October 1993. http://www.fas.org/man/docs/bur/part01.htm.

Begert, Lt Gen William J. "Kosovo and Theater Air Mobility." *Aerospace Power Journal* 13, no. 4 (Winter 1999): 11–21. http://www.airpower.maxwell.af.mil/airchronicles/apj/apj99/win99/begert.pdf.

Bellflower, Capt John W. "The Indirect Approach." *Armed Forces Journal*, January 2007, 12–16, 37–38.

"Biographies." *Air Force Link*. http://www.af.mil/bios.

Bossert, Col Phil. "Global War on Terror (GWoT): The Tipping Point for Air Mobility." *Airlift Tanker/Quarterly* 14, no. 4 (Fall 2006): 18. http://www.atalink.org/atq/ATQ_Fall_2006.pdf.

Bowen, Wyn Q., and David H. Dunn. *American Security Policy in the 1900s—Beyond Containment*. Brookfield, VT: Dartmouth Publishing Company, 1995.

Brown, Shannon A. "The Sources of Leadership Doctrine in the Air Force." *Air and Space Power Journal* 16, no. 4 (Winter 2002): 37–45. http://www.airpower.maxwell.af.mil/airchronicles/apj/apj02/win02/Win02.pdf.

Bryant, Jordan. "Airlift's Wild Ride—Already Stressed Crews Face a Stern New Test." *Air Force Times*, 22 January 2007. http://www.airforcetimes.com/issues/stories/0-AIRPAPER-2476994.php.

BIBLIOGRAPHY

Cassidy, Gen Duane H. Transcript of oral history interview by Dr. James K. Matthews and Margaret J. Nigra. Scott AFB, IL: USTRANSCOM Office of History, October 1998.

Chow, Brian G. *The Peacetime Tempo of Air Mobility Operations: Meeting Demand and Maintaining Readiness.* Santa Monica, CA: RAND Corporation, 2003. http://www.rand.org/pubs/monograph_reports/2005/MR1506.pdf.

Clausewitz, Carl von. *On War*, Edited and translated by Michael Howard and Peter Paret. Princeton, NJ: Princeton University Press, 1976.

Corum, James S., and Wray R. Johnson. *Airpower in Small Wars: Fighting Insurgents and Terrorists.* Lawrence: University Press of Kansas, 2003.

Crowl, Philip A. "Alfred Thayer Mahan: The Naval Historian." In *Makers of Modern Strategy: From Machiavelli to the Nuclear Age.* Edited by Peter Paret. Princeton, NJ: Princeton University Press, 1986.

CY 1998–CY 2006 AMC colonel promotion results briefing slides. Scott AFB, IL: Headquarters AMC/A1.

Danskine, Maj Wm. Bruce. "Fall of the Fighter Generals: The Future of USAF Leadership." Thesis, School of Advanced Airpower Studies, Maxwell AFB, AL, June 2001.

Downing, Lt Col (sel) Glen R. "The Mobility Air Forces: Unifying Culture for Contemporary Challenges." Fort Leavenworth, KS: School of Advanced Military Studies, Army Command and General Staff College, 2005.

Drew, Col Dennis M. "We Are an Aerospace Nation." *Air Force Magazine* 73, no. 11 (November 1990): 32–36.

Fabey, Michael. "African Command Good First Step, Expert Says." *Aerospace Daily and Defense Report*, 3 January 2007. http://www.aimpoints.hq.af.mil.

Federal Aviation Administration. "Aviation System Capacity Annual Report." Washington, DC: Federal Aviation Administration, Office of System Capacity and Requirements, 1993. http://ntl.bts.gov/lib/000/500/546/asc_93.pdf.

Federal Aviation Administration Air Traffic Organization. "Moving America Safely." http://www.faa.gov/library/reports/media/APR_year2.pdf.

Fogleman, Gen Ronald R. Transcript of oral history interview by Dr. James K. Matthews and Dr. John W. Leland. Scott

AFB, IL: USTRANSCOM, Air Mobility Command, March 1995.

———. "Verbatim: The Aerospace Nation." *Air Force Magazine* 79, no. 3 (March 1996). http://www.afa.org/magazine/march1996/03verb96.asp.

Garamone, Jim. "DoD Establishing U.S. Africa Command," 6 February 2007. http://www.defenselink.mil/News/NewsArticle.aspx?id=2940.

"GBU-43/B 'Mother of All Bombs' MOAB—Massive Ordnance Air Blast Bomb." *GlobalSecurity.org.* http://www.globalsecurity.org/military/systems/munitions/moab.htm.

Global Transportation Network. https://www.gtn.transcom.mil/public/home/aboutGTN/index.jsp.

Handy, Gen John W. Transcript of oral history interview by Dr. James K. Matthews and Dr. Jay H. Smith. Scott AFB, IL: Air Mobility Command, 2006.

Hazdra, Maj Richard J. *Air Mobility: The Key to the United States National Security Strategy.* Fairchild Paper. Maxwell AFB, AL: Air University Press, 2001. http://www.maxwell.af.mil/au/aul/aupress/fairchild_papers/Hazdra/Hazdra.pdf.

Hebert, Adam J. "Air Mobility's Never-Ending Surge." *Air Force Magazine* 89, no. 9 (September 2006): 46–52. http://www.afa.org/magazine/Sept2006/0906airmobility.pdf.

History. Air Mobility Command, 1 June 1992–31 December 1994. Vol. 1, K323.01. USAF Collection. Air Force Historical Research Agency, Maxwell AFB, AL.

History. Air Mobility Command (Provisional), 15 January–31 May 1992. Vol. 1, K323.01. USAF Collection. Air Force Historical Research Agency, Maxwell AFB, AL.

Hockmuth, Catherine MacRae. "UAVs—The Next Generation." *Air Force Magazine* 90, no. 2 (February 2007): 70–74. http://www.afa.org/magazine/feb2007/0207UAV.pdf.

Howard, Michael. "The Concept of Air Power: An Historical Appraisal." *Air Power History* 42 (Winter 1995): 5–11.

Hutcheson, Keith A. *Air Mobility: The Evolution of Global Reach.* Vienna, VA: Point One, 1999.

Isenberg, David. "The U.S. Global Posture Review: Reshaping America's Global Military Footprint." *British American Security Information Council*, 19 November 2004. http://www.basicint.org/pubs/Notes/BN041119.htm.

BIBLIOGRAPHY

Johnson, Gen Hansford T. Transcript of oral history interview by Dr. James K. Matthews and Dr. Jay H. Smith. Scott AFB, IL: USTRANSCOM Office of History, December 1992.

Kenner, Maj Regan. "Talking Paper on Air Force Intern Program (AMC)." Scott AFB, IL: Headquarters AMC/A1FD, 5 February 2007.

Krisinger, Capt Chris J. "Operation Nickel Grass: Airlift in Support of National Policy." *Airpower Journal* 3, no. 1 (Spring 1989): 16–28. http://www.airpower.maxwell.af.mil/airchronicles/apj/apj89/spr89/krisinger.html.

Kross, Gen Walter. "Air Mobility Symposium Address." In *Air Mobility Symposium: 1947 to the Twenty-first Century*. Washington, DC: Government Printing Office, 1998.

———. Transcript of oral history interview by Dr. James K. Matthews and Mr. Robert T. Cossaboom. Scott AFB, IL: USTRANSCOM Office of History, October 1999.

Lake, Anthony. "From Containment to Enlargement." Lecture. Johns Hopkins University School of Advanced International Studies, 21 September 1993. http://www.mytholyoke.edu/acad/intrel/lakedoc.html.

Larsen, Randell J. "Air Mobility Culture: A Re-Examination." *Mobility Forum*, July/August 1997. http://www.findarticles/com/p/articles/mi_qa3744/is_199707/ai_n8759468.

Lubold, Gordon. "Forward Surge!—Bush Plan: Iraqi Cooperation, and Early, Longer Deployments." *Army Times*, 22 January 2007. http://www.armytimes.com/issues/stories/0-ARMYPAPER-2478258.php.

Mahan, A. T. *The Influence of Sea Power upon History, 1660–1783*. Boston: Little, Brown, 1890.

McDowell, Col William L., Jr. "Mahan, Sea Power, and Air Power in 1953." Maxwell AFB, AL: Air War College, 1953.

Mets, Dr. David R. "Between Two Worlds: Fodder for Your Professional Reading on Global Reach and Air Mobility." *Aerospace Power Journal* 16, no. 1 (Spring 2002): 41–56. http://www.airpower.maxwell.af.mil/airchronicles/apj/apj02/spr02/spr02.pdf.

———. "Fodder for Your Professional Reading: Airpower and the Sea Services." *Airpower Journal* 13, no. 2 (Summer 1999):

67–84. http://www.airpower.maxwell.af.mil/airchronicles/apj/apj99/sum99/mets.pdf.

Mitchell, William. *Winged Defense: The Development and Possibilities of Modern Air Power—Economic and Military*. Mineola, NY: Dover Publications, 1988.

Nagl, John A. *Learning to Eat Soup with a Knife: Counterinsurgency Lessons from Malaya and Vietnam*. Chicago: University of Chicago Press, 2005.

Narvid, Lt Col Juan C. *Tanker-Force Structure: Recapitalization of the KC-135*. Maxwell Paper no. 32. Maxwell AFB, AL: Air University Press, 2004. http://aupress.maxwell.af.mil/Maxwell_papers/Text/mp32.pdf.

National Military Strategy of the United States. Washington, DC: Joint Chiefs of Staff, 1995. http://www.fas.org/man/docs/nms_feb95.htm.

The National Military Strategy of the United States of America: A Strategy for Today: A Vision for Tomorrow. Washington, DC: Joint Chiefs of Staff, 2004. http://www.defenselink.mil/news/Mar2005/d20050318nms.pdf.

National Security Strategy of the United States. Washington, DC: The White House, 1991. http://www.fas.org/man/docs/918015-nss.htm.

O'Hanlon, Michael E., Susan E. Rice, and James B. Steinberg. *The New Security Strategy and Preemption*. Policy Brief no. 113. Washington, DC: Brookings Institution, December 2002. http://www.brook.edu/comm/policybriefs/pb113/pdf.

Parrish, Noel F. "The Influence of Air Power upon Historians." USAFA Harmon Memorial Lecture no. 21. Colorado Springs, CO: United States Air Force Academy, 1978. http://www.usafa.af.mil/df/dfh/docs/Harmon21.doc.

Putrich, Gayle S. "USAF Reorganizing Intelligence Command." *DefenseNews*, 30 January 2007. http://integrator.hanscom.af.mil/2007/February/02012007/02012007-15.htm.

Quadrennial Defense Review Report. Washington, DC: Department of Defense, 6 February 2006. http://www.defenselink.mil/qdr/report/Report20060203.pdf.

Rosen, Stephen Peter. *Winning the Next War: Innovation and the Modern Military*. Ithaca, NY: Cornell University Press, 1991.

Rosine, SSgt Matthew. "Warfare Center Creates Mobility Warriors." Air Force Print News, 9 April 2006. http://www.af.mil/news/story_print.asp?id=123016991.

Schein, Edgar H. *Organizational Culture and Leadership.* San Francisco: Jossey-Bass Publishers, 1992.

Schulzinger, Robert D. *U.S. Diplomacy since 1900.* New York: Oxford University Press, 1998.

Seiler, Maj Michael. "Point Paper on Phoenix Hawk." Scott AFB, IL: Headquarters AMC/A1FD, 1 August 2006.

———. "Point Paper on Phoenix Horizon." Scott AFB, IL: Headquarters AMC/A1FD, 24 July 2006.

———. "Point Paper on Phoenix Mobility." Scott AFB, IL: Headquarters AMC/A1FD, 1 August 2006.

———. "Point Paper on Phoenix Reach." Scott AFB, IL: Headquarters AMC/A1FD, 1 August 2006.

Smith, James M. *USAF Culture and Cohesion: Building an Air and Space Force for the 21st Century.* Colorado Springs, CO: USAF Institute for National Security Studies, United States Air Force Academy, 1998.

Smith, Jay. *Anything, Anywhere, Anytime: An Illustrated History of the Military Airlift Command, 1941–1991.* Scott AFB, IL: Headquarters Military Airlift Command, 1991.

Sturkol, TSgt Scott T. "Warfare Center Is Now U.S. Air Expeditionary Center." Air Force Print News, 8 March 2007. http://www.af.mil/news/story_print.asp?id=123043713.

Thirtle, Dr. Mike. "Developing Aerospace Leaders for the Twenty-first Century: A Historical Context for the DAL Concept." *Aerospace Power Journal* 15, no. 2 (Summer 2001): 52–57. http://www.airpower.maxwell.af.mil/airchronicles/apj/apj01/sum01/thirtle.pdf.

Tirpak, John A. "Will We Have an Unmanned Armada?" *Air Force Magazine* 88, no. 11 (November 2005): 54–58. http://www.afa.org/magazine/nov2005/1105armada.pdf.

U.S. Air Force AIM Points. http://aimpoints.hq.af.mil (accessed 7 February 2007).

Vick, Alan J., Adam Grissom, William Rosenau, Beth Grill, and Karl P. Mueller. *Air Power in the New Counterinsurgency Era: The Strategic Importance of USAF Advisory and Assistance Missions.* Santa Monica, CA: RAND Corporation, 2006. http://www.rand.org/pubs/monographs/2006/RAND_MG509.pdf.

Weaver, Lt Col Nancy E. *Developing Aerospace Leaders for the Twenty-first Century.* Santa Monica, CA: RAND Corporation, April 2001. http://www.au.af.mil/au/awc/awcgate/au/weaver/pdf.

Whittle, Richard. "Built for War, Air Force Units Recap Peace." *Christian Science Monitor,* 1 December 2006.

Wilkes, Brig Gen Bobby J., Col Murrell F. Stinnette, and Maj Randall Reed. "Expeditionary Mobility Task Force: Projecting Combat Power." *Air and Space Power Journal* 19, no. 2 (Summer 2005): 15–22. http://www.airpower.maxwell.af.mil/airchronicles/apj/apj05/sum05/sum05.pdf.

Worden, Col Mike. *Rise of the Fighter Generals: The Problem of Air Force Leadership, 1945–1982.* Maxwell AFB, AL: Air University Press, 1998. http://aupress.maxwell.af.mil/books/Worden/Worden.pdf.

Worden, Maj Gen R. Mike. "A Changing of the Guard." *Air Force Magazine* 89, no. 7 (July 2006): 60–66. http://www.afa.org/magazine/July2006/0706guard.pdf.

Wynne, Hon. Michael W. "Letter to Airmen: Knowledge-Enabled Airmen," 12 March 2007. http://www.af.mil/library/viewpoints/secaf.asp?id=311.

After you have read this research report, please give us your frank opinion on the contents. All comments—large or small, complimentary or caustic—will be gratefully appreciated. Mail them to the director, AFRI, 155 N. Twining St., Maxwell AFB, AL 36112-6026.

The Rise of Air Mobility and Its Generals

Lenderman

Cut along dotted line

Thank you for your assistance.